EQUITY INSIGHT

ACHIEVING EQUITY IN EDUCATION WITH SOCIAL-EMOTIONAL LEARNING AND UNIVERSAL DESIGN FOR LEARNING

ETHAN CRUZ

CONTENTS

Introduction   v

1. TOXIC CULTURE OF EDUCATION   1
   Standardized Testing   2
   GPA and Ranking System   6
   The Influence of Teachers   8
   What it Takes to Change   12

2. WHAT IS EQUITY, AND WHY IS IT SO   17
   IMPORTANT?
   Importance of Equity   20
   Difference Between Equity and Equality   22
   Steps Towards Achieving Equity   24

3. LISTENING AS A TEACHER   30
   Best Practices for Effective Listening for   36
   Teachers
   Listening to Stakeholders   39

4. SOCIAL-EMOTIONAL LEARNING   41
   5 Pillars of Social-Emotional Learning   43
   EQ vs. IQ   47
   SEL and Equity in Schools   48
   Creating a SEL Program   51
   Program Effectiveness   53
   Assessment   56
   Potential Pitfalls   58
   Improving SEL with Students   60
   College and Career   64

5. UDL AND IMPLEMENTATION   67
   Representation   69
   Action and Expression   73
   Engagement   75

6. STRATEGIES AND PLANS   82
   Technology and Education   88
   Digital Distractions   90
   Building Equity   93
   Project-Based Learning   97
   Project Design   99
   Strategies for PBL   100
   After School Programs   102

7. TAKING ACTION   105
   Support   107
   Burnout   110
   Action Research   114
   Confidence   118

8. MAKING A REMARKABLE TEACHER   122
   Positive Mindset   126

   Conclusion   131
   Resources   137

INTRODUCTION

" "The principal goal of education in the schools should be creating men and women who are capable of doing new things, not simply of repeating what other generations have done; men and women who are creative, inventive, and discoverers, who can be critical and verify, and not accept, everything they are offered."
– Jean Piaget

You remember the excitement you got when you got your first teaching job. You're going to be a part of a school! You'll have built-in friends through coworkers and students. You decorate your classroom and make your lesson plans. You were so excited to see your students! Well, after a while, the school starts to tell you there is a change in curriculum because of an update to the standardized test. You feel like you're leaving out important information that can help the students learn more.

You adapt to standards because it's frowned upon if your class doesn't do well on the tests. You have one student who is very smart and sweet in class but isn't a successful test taker. She ends up failing the standardized test, so her motivation drops. She stops caring about her grades and lets her effort drop. You've seen this all happen in front of you, but you cannot change the grades of her test, even if you know how smart she is.

This feeling of helplessness runs strong in teachers. They may sense issues in a child's home life, and there could be nothing that they can do about it. They want to teach children more than what they are forced to fit into the curriculum. They want more freedom and control over their classroom.

Life in education can be fulfilling and exhausting. Educators consistently look out for their students. No matter their age, grade, education level, ethnicity, etc. Being a teacher means being selfless. You take time out of your life (even when you're not getting paid) to make sure everything is ready for your listeners. Teachers are the foundation of the education system. They are the most important aspect for improving the lives and learning experiences of students. The role of the teacher is to act as a light for students on a pathway of the unknown.

As a teacher, you have the opportunity to speak out about

flaws in the educational system, even if you don't know what they are right now, even if you aren't confident enough. The goal of this book is to show you, as teachers, why the education system isn't working. After reading, you'll be inspired to make changes for your students. Your goal, as a teacher, is to ultimately set your students up to be more prepared for life. You can do this by finding problems in your teaching experience and provide solid, thoughtful solutions and support.

The book will provide tools and examples to help you better understand how you can make a change. It will act as a map, guiding you through how to spot problems, how to break them down and create solutions, pitching and implementing changes, and how to use feedback. After reading, you are going to have an arsenal of tools that will improve the way you teach. This will give the students a better learning experience while practicing equity and being inclusive. If the students have a better experience, then the educational system as a whole will have a better experience. This leads to an improvement of equity in education. If you're interested in making a better education experience, you're perfect for this book for a number of reasons.

First, you are passionate. You love teaching. If you didn't, you would just quit, right? You stay for your students. Despite the problems you both face, despite the sacrifices you have to make, despite the shortfalls and failures. You know that your passion keeps you teaching, even when you feel challenged and disappointed by the education system.

This doesn't mean you've never wanted to quit. It just means that you love teaching enough to stick through the problems.

Second, you're an administrator or a school leader. These people are the ones that are in charge of a school, or they have a highly influential position. These people typically carry many responsibilities and have the ability to make important changes. School leaders and administrators Love new challenges and act as visionaries looking for ways to improve. The strongest school leaders are not afraid to make a change and are always on the lookout for the learners. Guidance counselors, superintendents, department heads, and more are included in this group.

Third, you have a disagreement with the education system. You have experienced issues, troubles, and complications associated with education. You know some of the trials and tribulations that are associated with getting an education, and you know something needs to change. In this case, you have the advantage of already knowing some of the problems that you think should be addressed. After all, the beginning of solving a problem starts with the problem itself. If we can't find the problem, we can't find the solution.

Fourth, you look far into the future of students. Many problems can be brushed under the rug and ignored. You stand apart by focusing on the long-term consequences. It can be easy to ignore a problem or pretend that it's not there. We tend to tell ourselves to believe what we want to believe. The hard part comes when we realize how big a problem is and know that we need to stop it. You tend to feel helpless, and you are looking for a way to make a change.

Fifth, you have coworkers and leaders who see teaching as work and not student-focused. As educational allies, we have to realize that without students, there are no teachers. If there is no one to teach, what is the teacher going to do? When people associated with education see their work as strictly professional, they tend to forget that they are affecting the lives of others. They are just clocking in and out for a paycheck.

As a teacher, it can be trying. You have to have your attention on your students, your work, meetings, family, personal matters, and the educational system as a whole. When you are being pulled and hundreds of directions at once, you can feel like you're about to break. When you reach this level of exasperation, you feel ready to quit. You might tell yourself to keep going and suck it up.

What if you were told that you don't have to suck it up? You can stand up for change and better the educational system no matter where you are. You can work through your problems with the school, administrators, and system to build motivation and fight the "giving up" mentality. As someone associated with education, it is our responsibility to be the voice for our learners. If we don't look out for them, how can we expect them to look out for themselves? If we aren't paying close attention to the students and learners, some will fall through the cracks.

Quality Teaching with Equity is going to focus on educational equity. Equity focuses on the measurement of fairness, opportunity, and achievement in education. Educational equity is important for every person that comes in contact with the system of education. The following pages will show you why equity is important, how to involve others to improve equity, and what factors affect equity.

The book is based on the research and personal experience of the author. The author was born in Mexico then moved to Texas when he was 12. He is a pioneer in education from his 13 years of teaching experience in grades kindergarten through 12th. He has now held a leadership position for the past four years. The author is dedicated to making education a better place for all students and teachers because the content is going to help students become better people in the real world. The author is writing this book because he understands there are many flaws in the education system and wants to bring attention to techniques and examples that can motivate teachers to aspire to be what students really need.

The author wants to show you what you are capable of. In our work, we can often perceive that we aren't important enough to cause change or our opinion doesn't matter enough to make a difference. The book is going to unlock your inner potential and show you the power that you hold. If you are going to make all of these changes, the first thing to do is understand the toxic culture of education.

TOXIC CULTURE OF EDUCATION

*T*he public education system has the tendency to convince students that if they do not go to college, then they won't be successful. This can be a motivation for the students to want to go to college. However, college isn't for everyone. Because the public schools push college so hard on the students, when the students believe they won't be able to make it in college, they automatically assume that they will be unemployed or try to find illegal work. It seems that the public education system is giving the children two options: college or failure.

This doesn't include the students who are musicians, poets, or those who want to work in a trade. It especially doesn't include the students who don't want to pursue college. It also discourages the students who can't go to college, whether it be for financial or academic reasons. As a child, students are told they can be whatever they want to be, but when they get older, they are told that they have to go to college or they aren't going to be successful. Students are so worried about grades, high-stakes testing, and college credits that they don't take the time to actually learn.

One major problem in the school system is they crush individuality. Students are asked to conform to the group and the chosen curriculum, techniques, environments, and much more. Being an individual in this system gets you left behind. It's important for students to be able to have an identity and anonymity. An identity is important for them to understand themselves, and anonymity is important for helping them work together with groups and society.

STANDARDIZED TESTING

High test scores are pushed hard on the teachers and students. Standardized testing is used to determine whether a school is "successful" or not. These tests determine a lot about a school, such as the intelligence of the students, competence of the teachers, availability, use of resources, and much more. This is a lot of pressure put on both the teachers and the students. Students who are younger, even in kindergarten, are taught that if they fail a test, they are a failure. These young children begin to realize that if they aren't good at standardized testing, they will not be good in school.

Standardized testing aims to measure the intelligence of students. Intelligence, however, is dynamic and is made up of many factors more than just what can be circled on a test. Intelligence is moldable and should be measured in more ways than one. Intelligence is different for everyone and cannot always be accurately measured and students. The testing system puts more emphasis on scores and grades than they do on learning and retention. An "A" on a test is simply a letter. It means nothing if the student cannot apply the knowledge to real life. It's as though children are measured as demographics. They transfer student knowledge into data.

Standardized tests also don't take into account the students' effort and motivation. If a student does the score as well, but they tried really hard, they are still seen as a failure by the test. The school forces students to be performance-oriented. They are motivated by grades and scores. It is best if a student approaches class with a mastery-oriented motivation. The student encounters the class with interest and curiosity for the content. They are going to be more internally motivated to listen and do well. When performance-oriented students need motivation, they look for external factors. It can be dangerous to depend on external factors for motivation because it can be troublesome when they aren't there.

Schools don't recognize that intelligence comes from many parts of life. They believe that intelligence is measured through grades. You cannot focus on grades only when you are trying to determine if a student is intelligent. A student could have all A's, but it could simply be because they can accurately memorize information for a test. Or they may just be a good test taker. They may not actually be more intelligent than someone who has B's and C's.

It's especially sad for students who have learning disabilities, test anxiety, are homeless and hungry, or distracted by abuse at home, or bullies at school. If something happens to alter the students testing ability, even for just the testing day, then they may be grouped together and kept separate from the students who scored higher. This is like putting a group of students in remedial math and having an honors math class. Or celebrating the high test scores of some students at a pep rally but making the students who didn't score as well on the test are left behind in the classroom.

It's ironic that schools preach "No child left behind," but with standardization, there are many children who are left behind. Standardization is the attempt to put schools into black or white categories. Either they are smart, or they aren't. Either they are successful, or they aren't. These tests don't account for the non-cognitive behavioral factors that can determine if a child is a success. Being kind, socially appropriate, friendly, and communicative are all signs that a child is growing to be a success. Standardized tests, however, don't test for these aspects.

Maybe a student was hungry from having no dinner last night, or immigrant children who don't speak very much English take the test and score poorly. In reality, they are very smart and well-rounded students, but because they scored poorly on a test, they are going to be seen as inept. In a study focusing on test anxiety in young children, the majority of students reported having more test anxiety during high-stakes tests versus normal classroom tests (Segool, Carlson, Goforth, Embse, Barterian, 2013). Not only do these students look like they aren't as successful as their peers, but the teachers can also be under pressure if the test scores aren't high enough.

The flaws in the education system need to be fixed because they are used to mold and develop the next generation. If we have hope for a successful future, then we need to prepare the next generation to take over. If schools will not allow students to learn through experience or explore their passions, how do they expect students to find out what they really love? Schools are more focused on assignments and projects than they are on exposing the student to real life.

Students are all directed to conform to structured guidelines. There is not much room for flexibility or self-expression. Imagine a professional dancer. She started out at a normal public school but couldn't seem to keep up with the other students because she wasn't able to learn as quickly as them. However, she learned better when she used her body and movement. As you know, students must sit stationary at a desk without talking or making noise to listen and learn from the teacher. She switched to a dance school where she successfully finished her studies and became a professional dancer. What if she had sat at that desk and conformed to the school standards and convinced herself that she was a failure because she couldn't score well on a test?

Schools are extremely controlling over what, when, where, and how students learn. They determine how long students study each subject, what they need to cover in each class, what they need to complete to pass, and just about everything else you can think of regarding students and learning. This means that, as a student, if you don't fit perfectly into the mold, then you're going to either be classified as a failure or forced to conform to the rigid school guidelines. The education system puts so much pressure on teachers and students that everyone is sent scrambling, trying to get everything done and done correctly. Some students are lost in this chaos, and others lose themselves.

In real life, people grow and learn at their own pace. They make mistakes, and they have successes, and they learn just as much from both. How does the education system expect all students to learn a certain way? If students had more freedom and control over their learning, then their passion for learning could flourish. If the system continues to force students to learn a certain way and learn a certain thing, then it can extinguish their love for learning. Even if they try really hard, they are told they are a failure if they don't do well on a test. This sets up the students' self-confidence for failure.

GPA AND RANKING SYSTEM

It is cruel that making one failing grade can slam the GPA, but it takes more than one good grade to bring the GPA back to where it was. If a student does poorly on one unit, they may work to the bone in that next lesson to make sure they get a better grade. They stay up late into the night and focus on just that one class, so they can make up their grade. Students must prioritize that class over others and can cause the student to miss out on other academic opportunities. The students' other studies could also be harmed by their stress and avoidance.

Because they have had to work so hard to bring up their grade, if they get a good grade the next week, they may decide to take it easy because they are exhausted from the week before. Let's say they get another bad grade that week; the next week, they are going to have to try hard. Then the next week, they are burned out. There's a never-ending cycle that is harmful to the students' mental and academic health.

The GPA of a student is meant to describe their academic performance. It only takes into account grades and how much the class is worth. It doesn't accurately capture the students' worth and knowledge. Self-determination, knowledge of working the system, and perseverance are what is actually shown by the GPA. GPA is more associated with self-discipline rather than intelligence itself. The part of the brain that is associated with self-discipline does not fully develop until the mid-20s. So, the GPA system is essentially testing skills in children that will take decades to master.

In order to fit into the GPA in the ranking system, students must pick specific classes with specific weights in order to improve their GPA or their rank. These students are restricted from taking classes that they want or are interested in because they are focused on raising their GPA and rank. Schools make it so important to have a high GPA and a higher rank for college. When in reality, GPA and class rank do not accurately determine intelligence. Class ranks pit the students against each other and make it a competition to see who can come in first. Because the ranking system makes it competitive, students will do whatever they can to raise their GPA.

The prevalence of cheating in school has drastically increased from the past. Students who are struggling in school cheat to make a good grade to pass. They are so overwhelmed with passing that they can't take the time to learn the material. Even the more successful students admit to cheating when it can give them a better grade. Why would the education system force these students to worry so much about a grade that they would cheat their way through? Isn't it counterproductive to make the students focus more on a grade than on learning the content?

THE INFLUENCE OF TEACHERS

As a teacher, you feel pressure from the administrators and the school leaders as well as pressure from your students. Teachers are the middleman and the messengers that get the blunt force of changes and tough situations. Students can complain to their teachers or choose not to participate if there is something they don't like. It is hard to recognize that teachers cannot control everything, and they may not be able to entertain the students' ideas because of restrictions they have. They might not have enough funding for materials or enough time for certain parts of the curriculum.

Teachers are consistently blamed for students' failure. If a student doesn't learn enough, it's because the teacher didn't explain enough. If a student is stressed out, it's because a teacher assigns too much work. Teachers can absolutely affect the learning of a student, but the teacher is not always the problem. Sometimes it is not the teacher nor the student that is the problem, but it's the system that's negatively influencing these students.

Teachers are forced to be part of the bureaucracy. They can't control curriculum, testing, or standards. They don't have a lot of flexibility when it comes to what they teach and how they teach it. But they are quick to be blamed when something goes wrong. The teachers have to make it work with whatever worksheets and materials they are given, even if they don't think they are effective. Teachers are expected to prepare students for tests that can't effectively test all students' abilities. Because of the idea that teachers are to blame when students don't do well, it has led to suggestions such as student-performance-based compensation and merit pay. The teachers are just as oppressed as the students when it comes to creativity with learning. The system has a way of crushing creativity.

Throughout all this time, trials, tribulations, and trouble, it can be easy for teachers to blame themselves. Many teachers get discouraged and angry because they may know that their students aren't prepared for the next grade, but there's nothing that they can do because they don't have the time or the resources they need to accurately teach the students.

Throughout everything, however, teachers are often one of the most powerful parts of the education system. Teachers often don't realize the influence and power they have because they are blinded by what the administration wants. The unique opportunity of seeing the administration's direct effects on the students firsthand lies in the hands of teachers. Teachers also have the ability to get close to the students. A teacher will be able to better determine a student's intelligence than a test can because they know that student personally. They understand that one student might read slow, but they are excellent in math. Teachers realize that while one student doesn't do great on their grades, they are very funny and have some great work experience.

Teachers also experience pressure from extracurriculars, sports, and parents. In many situations, teachers feel pressured to inflate grades because of the risk of a football player not playing on Friday or a student not getting into an Ivy League school because of a low grade. They may be feeling pressure to simply pass a student because they can't seem to understand a concept, and they don't have the time to work with the student one on one.

Out-of-field teaching is also a common problem in school systems due to the lack of resources. Some teachers may be forced to teach subjects that they aren't specifically trained in because they have no one else. This can affect the entire learning process in the classroom. Now the teacher has to adapt to the content and can't properly focus on the students or their teaching techniques.

If the school doesn't do as well as they had hoped or planned on standardized testing, then teachers may be subject to certain training or courses. Teacher incompetence is said to be measured by the students' ability to score high on a test. Even if the teacher was great and did everything they were supposed to, if the students across the school don't score well, the teachers may have to attend a weekend training or do some type of online courses in an attempt to raise overall test scores. This is harmful to the teachers' self-esteem because they may think they are doing a good job, but the education system and standardized tests are telling them something different. Because of the inability of standardized tests to accurately measure students' intelligence, there is no true way to determine if a teacher is doing well or not.

These teachers try their hardest even though they are under a broken system. They work countless hours every day to make sure their classroom is orderly. These hours don't amount up to their salary. Starting out as a teacher, you can expect the salary to be between $30,000 - $50,000 even though they have all completed some college work and commonly work 60+ hours a week. This desperately needs to change.

WHAT IT TAKES TO CHANGE

When teachers realize their true power, they can group together and make serious changes in the school system. Teachers have the ability to see the situation from the students' perspective and administrations. All people in the education system can work together to see what it takes to make a change. You should all be motivated to make the changes.

In order to make a change, educational leaders need to be internally motivated. Teachers often get very emotionally involved with their students and in their teaching experiences. Use this as motivation to want to seek out problems in your system and create solutions for them. The motivation that comes from within is much stronger than external motivation. With the school system being so strict, it's hard to find external motivation. When these educational leaders unlock their inner motivation, they can be unstoppable.

We need good leadership to implement these solutions into the education system. Leaders who are brave and are willing to guide the path for others. Leaders who have the students in mind and what is going to be best for them. Leaders, regardless of the job title, act as pioneers for a new way of life. Being a leader means being willing to take that first step that way everyone can follow.

Followers are just as important as leaders. Although the leaders take that first step, it's important for the followers to be close behind. The support of you all working together is going to be like an army. Followers support the leader just as the leader supports the followers. When there is such strong teamwork, you are going to achieve your goal.

Teamwork is a very important aspect associated with making change. Making a unanimous decision is important for making sure that everyone feels heard. Teamwork means working together to achieve the same goal. Working as a team creates strength and a bond that is harder to break by external factors. Support is very strong, and teamwork can explode your productivity. Teams have more productivity than working alone. Teams will have more knowledge, diversity, thoughts, ideas, and opinions than when working alone.

Knowledge of the situation is vital to making change. When you don't know what needs to be changed, you won't be able to make a plan to change it. Seek out and find challenges in the education system and group with others to see what can be done to change it. Once you know where to start, you know where to finish. Now you just have to decide how you are going to get there.

Individuality is important for showing true intelligence. Since the school system aims to extinguish individuality, it can be inclusive to only some students. In order to improve individuality, we need to take a few steps to get there.

- Create a curriculum that allows students to show their knowledge, in more than just one way, to determine their intelligence.
- Focus on inclusive learning models regardless of other factors (socioeconomic status, access to technology, etc.).
- Include events and groups to support the children and families who have more barriers than others (poverty, health, home life, disabilities, etc.).

A curriculum where knowledge is measured in more than one way will determine the true test of intelligence. You cannot judge someone's intelligence by telling them to pick answers on paper. Everyone is different, and no one learns the exact same. Allow students to show more sides of themselves when being asked to show intelligence. It creates a better idea of the student as a whole. When you have more factors than one, you get a better overall look, and it's a more accurate description of knowledge. This could include a test, a hands-on experiment, and an interview. The education system needs to change its expectations for what students need to do with the information they are told.

Perhaps you want to make a lesson plan where you tell all

of your students to go home and design a website and bring it back to class for a grade. This would be fun for everyone and fun for you because you get to see the work that everyone has put in. Unfortunately, not all students have access to WiFi at home. Ensure you have the ability to allow those students to work on their websites during class instead of at home. You can give students the option: work on your website or complete an assignment. Make sure the assignment can be done at home or at school (like a worksheet). This allows you to still give your teaching presentation for that day (the worksheet), and you still let students use the internet to build their web pages.

Many low-income families experience troubles that others don't. They may be homeless, hungry, or needing the students to skip school to work. Immigrant children and their families may not speak excellent English. Students with disabilities may not have access to the resources they need for an easier educational experience. Try to host events to include these students and families. You could have a weekly meet-up for a few hours in the library where you serve food and open the school to any families who want to eat and sit in the library to study. You could host a weekly or monthly workshop for immigrant students and their families to attend to better understand English. You could allow the students with disabilities to stay longer after school or come in earlier, so they have more access to resources independently. Students with disabilities are also generally embarrassed, so giving them an opportunity to study one on one eases their barriers to education.

Overall, school leaders need to ask themselves: Is the school's purpose to develop or to choose and define a student's talents? By selecting students' talents, such as in the ranking system, they are advertising certain qualities about those students. If they were developing students' talents, they would be allowing them to explore themselves and let them, as well as you, figure out what they are good at. If a student is put into History as an elective, they may do poorly if they aren't well-versed in that subject. However, if you had let that student replace that elective with carpentry, then they would've probably gotten a better grade and a better GPA. But because the school focused on History instead of Carpentry, that student is now ranked lower in the class, holds a lower GPA, and seems "less intelligent" than their peers.

The inability of that student to find out what they were good at only showed them that they are bad at History. Instead of allowing the student to excel in a different class, they are deemed as a failure because they weren't successful in History. This sets children up with the mindset that they must succeed at everything they do or else they are a failure. Even if the student has all A's, and one C, their GPA will not reflect a perfect record. Why does the student have to be punished because they aren't as experienced in that one area?

2

WHAT IS EQUITY, AND WHY IS IT SO IMPORTANT?

The education system from K-12 can determine the rest of a person's life. If a person doesn't do well in school, then chances are they have a harder time doing well in life. Those who don't finish school or are left behind in the classroom tend to need more social support, have poor health and child welfare. A fair and equitable system is going to increase the opportunities of education and extend it to all students. The education system has the ability to reach all students. They are increasing human capital and can make society much more equitable. Equity in education will improve trust and social cohesion.

Equity is not only about race. It's about receiving the same advantages and opportunities between men and women. It's about improving the same opportunities between immigrant and native-born students. Equity is about bringing out the best in everyone, not just the smartest or the best test-takers. Equity involves aspects such as gender, family background, socioeconomic status, disability, culture, religious beliefs, sexual orientation, personality, and so much more.

When educators are learners, they act as students. They seek information, set aside space and time to discuss, and work with others to reach a solution. Educators are able to make solutions because they do an inventory of their own data, student experience, and beliefs. Educators as learners with good attitudes can help create a growth mindset.

It has been shown that a growth mindset can combat the effects of poverty on the achievement of students. Not only is a growth mindset beneficial for students, but it is beneficial for teachers alike. When teachers adopt a growth mindset, they are more open to identifying issues and will be more effective in solving the problems. When teachers have a growth mindset, they are a positive influence on their students. The chances are higher that students working with a teacher with a growth mindset also have a growth mindset. Social-emotional learning and diverse backgrounds also play a role in the creation of growth mindsets in students and teachers.

Social-emotional learning is the ability to appropriately operate in public and manage emotions. This type of learning is important for showing and feeling empathy for others, achieving and setting positive goals, creating relationships, and applying knowledge that they have received from previous experiences. Studies indicate that children of color have more barriers when interacting with social-emotional learning. If everyone improves their social-emotional learning, it can remove many barriers experienced by students. Improving social-emotional learning will improve equity.

IMPORTANCE OF EQUITY

Equity is important, especially in the educational system, because there are groups of people who receive privileges based on their identity and groups of people who are marginalized because of their identity. We already operate in an inequitable system in real life, but providing equity in the educational system can help students prepare for the inequity in the real world. Children learn at a young age when they are receiving different outcomes from their peers. Their opinions on these differences can be affected by the educational system. If the inequitable system deems margin-alized children as troublesome, then the child may believe that they are, in fact, troublesome. Them being tagged with this adjective so early in life can increase the chances that the child will actually become troublesome.

Equity shows students that although they may have more barriers than others, they can overcome them and be just as great as their counterparts. Equity teaches children that they can find the resources that they need in order to do great in life. When things are equal, children are given resources, and if it's not enough, they are told, "Well, everyone else got the same. I don't know why you can't make it work." This ignites frustration in the student that can lead to them feeling defeated and unimportant. These children can begin to despise others and blame themselves for not being as good as others. It's insulting to some children to insinuate that they all have the same resources, and they will all perform highly.

Students don't deserve this treatment, especially at a young age.

Equity is so important because our children deserve it. They start their life fresh and brand new, and they come to us to mold and develop them for the real world. With them being the next generation, it's our responsibility to create a sustainable and successful group of students. All students deserve the same opportunities to reach their goals. Often, these students are struggling with problems that aren't their own or that they can't control. Equity can help fill the gap between what a student has and what they need to be successful.

Equity can help appropriately mold a student to be successful in life. Equity shows students that while things may not always be fair, they can overcome their circumstances with the help of others. Equity shows that teamwork can improve the outcome. Multiple people working together to improve the learning experience of the student and the student will feel support. Now, they're more likely to perform better.

Equity improves participation from all parties. When everyone is given the same opportunity, more people are going to be able to take part. With equity, there could be less teacher turnover and fewer student dropouts. When participants see that they can capture and achieve their goals, they are going to be more self-confident. When people are more self-confident, they are more willing to put themselves out there and participate in situations.

Equity improves outcomes for schools, teachers, students, and more. With resources being allocated to where they are needed, the areas that are getting the resources are going to be able to accomplish their set goals. Equity improves human capital and will ultimately pay off in the end. Equity may make some people uncomfortable, but it is important to recognize this emotion so you can work past it and focus on the bigger picture. When students have equity, they are able to work past their obstacles and focus on the bigger picture.

DIFFERENCE BETWEEN EQUITY AND EQUALITY

Equity and equality sound the same, and they are typically used interchangeably. Both equity and equality are important in the education system. But when people think of equality, they think of being fair. Ironically, when there is more equity, things are more equal. Equity means elevating all students to the same level. Equality means being fair to all. When you are focused on equality, you are making sure that everyone gets the same treatment. When you are focused on equity, you make sure that everyone has the same opportunities and advantages. Equality focuses on the outcome, while equity focuses on the experience.

Equality focuses on giving everyone the same exact resources, while equity focuses on giving resources based on the recipients' needs. Think of a student who scores a 95 on a test and another score a 45. The majority of the class failed, so the teacher decided to add 5 points to all tests. This is great for the student who scored a 95 because now they have 100. For the other student, however, they still failed. It was equal to give everyone 5 points. But if the teacher wanted everyone to pass, she would need to increase each grade by the amount needed to reach a passing grade. Although it's not technically fair, all students will be equal in the fact that they all passed the test. While equality is beneficial, it doesn't address the needs of all students. Even when the school is considered equal, there are still students who struggle.

Equity and equality play a large role in school resource allocation. If it were a goal, all schools would get the same amount of funding. All schools could get the same amount of computers. All schools can get the same amount of textbooks. This doesn't account for the schools that have an excess in funding, and the students typically have all of their own computers, and they can afford to buy different textbooks. Then you have schools that don't have enough money, computers, or textbooks to pass around. Even though what both schools got was equal, the higher-class school was overflowing while the lower-class school was struggling.

When schools focus on equity, they are focusing on the needs of the students. They are taking into account each individual's experiences and circumstances when on the road to success. Equity is fair, adaptable, and individual-focused. The quality is great, focused, equal, and generic. Every student learns differently. When you take a group-focused mindset, you are leaving behind those students that don't fit into the group. When teachers and schools can provide equity, they are giving students the opportunity to reach the same level of aspirational goals.

Not only are our schools and teachers beneficial for equity, but so are our students, parents, and the community. Parents can improve equity by ensuring their child gets the resources to achieve equity. If a student is not doing so well in math, the parent can get a tutor. This can give the child the same advantages as another at achieving a good test score. The community can work with the school to provide the resources needed to achieve equity. A health clinic could offer general services to students who don't have insurance. A local shelter can provide a place to stay for children who don't have one. A restaurant could host a fundraiser to get more resources for disabled students. When everyone works together, it can be possible to achieve equity in the education system.

STEPS TOWARDS ACHIEVING EQUITY

1. Know who your students are. Listen to more stories from your students. Get to know them on a deeper level than just academia. Find out what they like and don't like. Find out where they're from and what their favorite thing is to eat. The more you learn about them, the better you can

tailor and differentiate instruction throughout your classroom.

2. Be someone who politely demands the best from their students. Convince the students how smart they are and show them what they're capable of. This gentle but stern push forces the students to dig within and reach high goals. Taking an equity-focused approach allows us to set high expectations and commit to each child's success.

3. Use your students' stories to create their learning stories. You can learn a lot about a child from the stories they tell. You can see how they approach problems, how they feel about themselves, and how quickly they are to learn.

4. Be flexible in your instruction. Some of your students may need special attention, and others may not understand a certain topic. If you had plans to move further with the content, but the majority of your class doesn't understand that certain topic, then you need to be able to take the time to go back and reassess. Be prepared for situations where you need to change your instruction.

5. Make the students comfortable with failure. If a student fails, they can feel ashamed and want to suffer in silence or act out and disobey. It teaches students that failure is an opportunity to learn what doesn't work. Show them that when they fail,

they are actually learning. This sets them up for a lifetime of positive encounters with being unsuccessful.

6. Embrace and celebrate culture. Diversity is an accelerant for creativity. The vast cultures and ideas, thoughts, and opinions create the perfect environment for diversity. This diversity leads to a wide range of ideas and discussions due to more perspectives on the situation.

7. Be vigilant. Look for opportunities where you can improve equity. Take chances when you see those opportunities. Be brave enough to step up and make the change when you know it can improve equity. This will be what it truly means when you say no child left behind.

8. Improve communication between all parties associated with equity. Make sure the teachers and educational leaders can speak with the parents and vice versa. Make sure the students can communicate with the community and vice versa. The more communication you have, the more clearly all parties will be able to see the situation. With more clarity, there's less of a chance of mistakes and misunderstanding and a higher chance of success.

Studies show that the structure of education systems can affect equity. When education sorts students by attainment, it can cause inequities and inequalities, especially when done in early childhood or early learning stages. Education systems need to be re-designed in a way that is strong for all students from beginning to end. Early tracking of academic performance needs to be reevaluated and justified. Even waiting to sort students until an older age can improve outcomes and reduce inequities and inequalities. Education systems need to be changed to take an equity-focused approach.

Class requirements should be more flexible and diverse. The students need to experience multiple situations so they can determine what they like and what they don't like. Finding an interest in high school improves the chances of that student carrying on with that interest throughout their life. Whether they get an interest in automotive or in business, the students have the opportunity to experience that and understand that they enjoy it. More diverse class requirements would increase interaction between students and new situations.

The curriculum needs to include and promote more formative assessments. A formative assessment includes giving feedback about performance to a student, and then the student and teacher adapting in response to the outcomes. Both the teacher and the student will be able to see areas that need to be improved or that can be altered to be more beneficial. The formative assessment highlights the trouble areas and downfalls that a student is experiencing. This one-on-one work improves the equity in schools and classrooms.

Homework needs to be justified because it doesn't always allow for equity. While homework is equal, not all students have the resources at home that others do in order to be able to get a better grade. Some students may be homeless or lack parental support to get help for their homework. Some students may work and forget homework assignments or be too tired to think through them clearly, or stay up late to get them done and end up doing poorly. The student-athletes also have trouble when having to do practice and homework. Depending on homework to improve performance can hurt some students. If anything, homework can be used as a second chance to learn, not to deliver and evaluate new material.

The curriculum needs to reflect a more real-life approach. Classes focused on working in corporate America, entrepreneurship, filing taxes, finance, and budgeting would be much more beneficial to some students than carpentry or calculus. When curriculum takes a more real-life-based approach, it allows the students to prepare for more than just college and career. Students spend so much of their time choosing between college and career that they don't have the ability to find themselves or figure out exactly what it is they want to do. This approach allows students the knowledge to avoid mistakes they could make in their early 20s. They could learn how to be independently wealthy, so they don't necessarily have to do a career or college. The real world includes a lot more than college or a career. Providing more attractive alternatives can prevent the failure of some students.

Educational resources need to ensure that the money is going towards equity-based components. It can be hard for many schools to find funding or get more money to increase the resources to improve equity. So, it's important to look at the current financials of the school to determine where money can be reallocated. The funding may be altered to focus more on equity. There may even be solutions that improve equity and save money.

3

LISTENING AS A TEACHER

Teachers have the opportunity to learn just as much from children as they do from their teachers. It's obviously important for the student to listen to the teacher, but it's also important for the teacher to listen to the student. Listening to the student can allow the teacher to make a better connection, figure out problems that the student is experiencing, and find ways where the students can improve and how they can improve. Listening does not mean hearing. Hearing a student is listening to them say they don't understand something. Listening is hearing them say they don't understand a topic for three weeks in a row.

Listening is critical to good communication. When one person is delivering all of the information and not listening to the other, it can dampen effective communication. Listening to, and delivering material, are required for successful communication. Teachers should make listening just as important as teaching. Teachers should have good listening skills, creating stronger connections with the students, and being more empathetic. Listening improves the ability to negotiate with students and defuse classroom conflicts. Listening not only improves the classroom environment and the relationship between teacher and student, but it also improves academic and performance outcomes.

As a teacher, you do most of the talking. And as the student, they do most of the listening. Listening skills are important for both teacher and student, and both parties need to learn to respect the other. Fortunately, listening skills can be learned and improved. In order to better understand listening, it can be broken down into stages. True listening starts with lowering your guard and trying to receive the message that the speaker is trying to deliver.

When you are getting ready for a listening experience, try to let your guard down and drop your defenses. Many times, we can let past experiences affect how listening skills are in various environments. Once we sit down in a work meeting, we may tune out because the last two meetings were boring. If someone we don't like is speaking, it can be hard to move our emotions out of the way so we can hear what they're saying. Starting a listening experience with a bad attitude will taint the entire interaction. You must at least be willing to listen, even if you don't want to.

Listening means you need to do more than hear what they say. You need to capture the emotions of the speaker.

You need to understand the seriousness and the tone of the speaker. You ultimately want to make sure that you understand what the speaker is trying to tell you. It's important to understand that different words have different meanings between people. What do you think means one thing, your speaker could mean something else. That's why it's important to take in more stimuli than just the words they are saying.

Try to listen with full attention. Hold judgment, criticism, and assumptions for the end of the story. You don't want to interrupt or jump to conclusions before the student finishes the story because you could upset them or cause them to lose their train of thought. This can lead to a longer interaction and possible irritation between both parties. It's common to judge people based on our own information and experiences mentally. This can negatively affect what they are trying to say, so if we jump to conclusions, we could convince ourselves that they are saying something that they actually aren't. When you are an unskilled listener, you only hear the words you want to hear.

Now is the time to focus on a response. This is where you show that you have actually been listening. Give your speaker assurance that you were listening to them with full attention. This is a very important part of constructive listening. Feedback can be given in the form of asking for more information or clarity and giving some visual acknowledgment such as nodding, frowning, or smiling. Making small gestures and remarks during the presentation also shows you were attentive. You can occasionally nod your head and say simple replies such as, "Oh wow," and "Okay."

It's important for both parties to understand that there are obstacles to listening. There will be internal obstacles as well as external obstacles. Internal obstacles include any reason inside the body as to why someone cannot listen. This can be the previous negative conceptions and ideas that we discussed earlier. It can also be the inability to focus, racing thoughts, attention disorders, and a small attention span. Many people with these issues can learn to recognize when their mind has drifted away and bring it back to attention. Internal obstacles for children include confusion, inability to understand, or lack of interest in the topic.

External factors that negatively affect listening include noise. Noise can be considered any external factor that prevents the listener from active listening. Noise can be considered audible such as construction noise, traffic, someone's phone going off, a classroom full of kids speaking, and more. Noise can be visual. Visual noise can be people walking in and out of the room, the listener moving their body too much, poor lighting, and much more. Noise can also be physical, such as uncomfortable clothing or lack of seating. Lastly, noise can be smell such as a fish dinner, walking past the bathroom, or the smell of a nice air freshener can all bring our attention away from the speaker.

In both situations, it can be difficult to actively listen for the entire time that the speaker is talking. It's important to make allowances when there is poor listening and instead work towards fixing it. This is why we notice when our mind wanders, so we bring it back to paying attention. Listening can also be hard in terms of anxiety, boredom, and tension. For some people, this can be debilitating and can prevent them from learning, participating, and listening in the classroom.

Language barriers are also a strong predictor of poor communication. Many classrooms now have at least some students who come from non-English-speaking backgrounds. Students who use English as a second language can find it harder to comprehend and therefore find it harder to listen. Communication may be a little more difficult when there is a language barrier; however, when the parties take their time to work together, they can come up with solutions that will make listening and teaching easier for both sides.

Attitudes, words, and tone can also affect listening. After being at school for seven hours, a day students are going to lose their concentration. Their mental energy will be depleted; they could be hungry or thirsty, tired, disturbed, or just distracted by something they have personally going on. This is the perfect opportunity to move away from planned activities and take a brief time to re-energize the group. It can help them relax a little, which will improve their focus and improve learning.

When teachers take part in empathetic listening, they have a better ability to understand the feelings and emotions of another person. This can be a way to gain the perspective of your speaker. Empathy can come easier when you have personally experienced the same situation or feeling as someone else. Being empathetic means understanding the emotions behind the words and connecting with them. Sharing these emotions at the same time can improve empathy and therefore improve relationships. It can be hard for students and teachers alike to empathize with the opposing view.

Character differences, personality clashes, the status gap, socioeconomic classes, gender, cultural, and age differences may act as barriers to effective listening. This can be over-come by showing true willingness to listen and understand the other party. In the classroom, empathetic listening involves:

- Reducing hostility and tension between the student and teacher.
- Promoting honest communication and building confidence and trust.
- Giving the teacher and student time to clarify their thinking
- Improving the students' self-respect and niceness towards the teacher.
- Keeping communication open, active, and alive.

BEST PRACTICES FOR EFFECTIVE LISTENING FOR TEACHERS

A genuine interest in listening is going to be the best way to get someone to listen. You can still get someone to listen through other ways, but everyone is different. That is why it is important for teachers to listen, so they know how their students are going to listen best. Respecting privacy and being patient are also important in active listening.

If you are trying to rush through what someone is saying, it will dampen the message and negatively influence communication. Respecting privacy is also ensuring that you aren't being too intrusive. Being intrusive means asking private questions or asking for more information once the speaker has already said they don't want to divulge any more. Don't push the speaker to give more information than they want because it could end communication altogether. It can also show that you are more interested in what you don't know instead of what this speaker is saying.

Don't belittle or undercut another person's feelings. Saying things like you're making this a big deal or it's not that serious can make a person's feelings seem invalid. If someone comes to you to talk about something and they feel rejected, it is going to damage that communication and interaction and all interactions in the future. Even if it doesn't seem important, it could be crucial to the learning of the student.

Create a safe environment with open body language. You

don't want to sit facing away from the student, with your arms crossed, looking down. This can make the student feel unheard, and they may not want to come to you in the future. Turn towards the student, lift up your chin, and make eye contact. This will show the student that you are listening and you are open to communication. It will make the student feel important, which will make communication easier.

Taking a break is sometimes critical for listening to students. Teachers care a lot. This is great for developing motivation to make positive changes for students, but it also leaves the teacher open to be hurt. Teachers can get angry and aggravated at their students the same way students can get angry and aggravated at their teachers. Saying cross words and making insults could completely ruin a relationship. When it feels as though you cannot listen because you are too angry, pause the situation and take a break. Step into the hallway or send the student into the hallway and collect your thoughts before attempting to listen to them. Your anger will be pitted against their anger, and there will be no chance of listening on either side. Neither side will feel heard, and the situation will just escalate.

Staying calm in a heated listening situation can determine whether the outcome will be good or bad. When there is active and empathetic listening, it can decrease conflict and de-escalate any situation. If there is an argument between two students, the teacher can act as a liaison. The teacher can fully and quietly listen to one story without bias and then repeat for all others involved in the predicament.

Having the ability to shut out the noise and listen to your students can potentially save them from hurting themselves, others, or their relationships.

Active listening for students also shows that it is respectful. When students feel as though they are being listened to, it is easier for them to listen to the teacher. It can also show them and teach them good listening skills that they can use throughout their lives. When students learn the importance of listening as a child, they are going to be able to harness benefits throughout their life that they wouldn't have been able to grasp before.

Listening to students is important for showing them that they are cared for. When students feel heard, they are more likely to participate in class and have higher grades. These students tend to be successful because they feel as though they are being included in the process. When you can include children in the process of their learning, they are going to be able to learn a lot easier. When learning has individualized, the possibilities for students are endless. Listening is critical for that individualization that students need.

Listening doesn't always have to be verbal. You can ask the students to write down any issues they may have anonymously or have them write votes on the board. Audible listening can be beneficial, but students may be more comfortable with anonymity when that trust hasn't yet been established.

LISTENING TO STAKEHOLDERS

Teachers get pressure from people all around them. They feel pressure from their students, their parents, and the administration. It can be hard to listen to someone if you feel threatened or attacked. Sometimes when a student isn't successful, the teacher may be blamed. However, most parents care about their child and their education, so they will reach out if their child isn't doing well in school.

A stakeholder is someone who has an interest in the child's education. It is someone who can affect the child's education, whether it be negatively or positively. It's important to listen to the positive stakeholders because they also want the best for the student. Stakeholders can say things that the student is unconscious of, or they feel embarrassed talking about it. Listening to stakeholders as a teacher can help you learn more about the student.

You may be able to understand the student better when you know their outside situation. Maybe a student is falling behind in reading because they have recently been diagnosed with migraines. A student could be stealing food from lunch because they won't eat that weekend. Listening to those involved in the students' education allows you to make a stronger connection with that student and understand the resources they need to be successful.

When these parents and family members reach out to teachers, teachers have a great opportunity of gaining another perspective on the education system. Teachers are able to see situations from the point of view of parents and family members. Gaining more perspective on the situation gives a teacher an overall better look at the bigger picture.

Stakeholders in a child's education are critical for helping the student succeed. This can include friends and family, legal guardians, staff from medical clinics or group homes, doctors or medical providers, and much more. If members of a group home reach out to a teacher because a student isn't being social, the teacher could set up a group project or activity. If an eye doctor says a child would see better from the front of the classroom, the teacher can arrange for the child to sit in the front. Listening to those involved in a child's life can help customize a child's learning.

People involved in children's lives see them through different lenses. A swim coach could see a student differently than a teacher. A parent will see sides of the student that a teacher never will. The more people involved in a child's education, the more support they will have. When they have these large groups of support, chances are higher they will succeed. So, listening to those who can help the child succeed can make a world of difference.

4

SOCIAL-EMOTIONAL LEARNING

A student comes into class with large circles around their eyes. They look exhausted, and they're dragging their feet. They walk past you as you hold out your hand for their big assignment. You can tell they look defeated. You realize they must've had a rough night, and that could be why they didn't get their assignment turned in. After class, you pull the student to the side and ask them what happened with their assignment. It turns out that the child's house had burned in a fire last week, and they've been staying with a friend where they don't get enough sleep. They left their project in their backpack at home. You allow them another day to turn in the paper without penalty. This is being emotionally intelligent.

Being emotionally intelligent means being able to recognize emotions. Whether these emotions be yours or others, emotional intelligence starts with being able to recognize your feelings. Many times, our bodies, faces, and minds can react to situations faster than we can think. This is because emotion can build up inside and shoot out at all times. Being emotionally intelligent changes the world. You could honk and yell at the person that cut you off, or you can catch yourself, realize you're angry, and try to work through it instead of blowing up.

Patience is a key to being emotionally intelligent. As you've probably seen, our emotions can happen in a millisecond. We have to give ourselves a bit of time to process and control our emotions. When we take a moment to complete a checklist of our emotions, we can prevent outbursts that are motivated by emotions. If you are getting irritated with another teacher at the end of the school day, stop and think to yourself: am I really upset with them, or am I tired from a long day? Maybe a colleague is being short with you. Instead of thinking, "They must be irritated with me, or I've done something wrong" or deciding that you don't like working with them, think about how they must be feeling right now. They could be physically tired or going through something in their personal life. When you're emotionally intelligent, you take in all parts of a situation, not just what you can see and hear.

When you're emotionally intelligent, you're looking below the surface. You see the reasons why people are upset, rather than just the fact that they are upset. You can look at the root of the problem and work to fix it instead of superficially arguing and name-calling. You can help other people work through their emotions when you're emotionally intelligent.

Perhaps a student gets angry while doing work in the classroom and becomes confrontational when asked about homework. You could see the child as disobedient or rude. When you take a moment to process their emotions, you may realize that they only get upset when talking about schoolwork. After a conversation with them (instead of disciplining them), you realize they've been dealing with dyslexia, but they were too scared to ask for help.

5 PILLARS OF SOCIAL-EMOTIONAL LEARNING

Social-emotional learning (SEL) is a critical part of human actions. Social-emotional learning is involved in education, human interactions, feelings, perceptions, the ability to make decisions, create and maintain relationships, empathy, and so much more. Social-emotional learning improves educational equity by:

- Creating important relationships between school, family, and community.
- Developing a healthy and successful learning environment.
- Improving instruction and curriculum.
- Encouraging ongoing evaluation, feedback, and re-evaluation.

Recent studies prove that social-emotional learning is responsible for helping people develop themselves into successful and high-functioning adults. SEL has been proven to:

1. Improve students' perceptions of school and in the classroom now and later.
2. Grow healthy skills, relationships, attitudes.
3. Increase academic performance in the short-term and long-term.
4. Aid long-term improvements in social behaviors.
5. Be a smart financial investment.
6. Decrease student's behavior problems, anxiety, and addiction.

There are five important parts to SEL (CASEL 5): self-awareness, social awareness, responsible decision-making, self-management, and relationship skills. These core competencies can be taught and modeled to children in all developmental stages. The CASEL 5 acts as a guide for using SEL to improve the lives of students. CASEL uses a systemic approach to show the importance of creating equity in education.

Self-awareness means having the ability to name and recognize our personal emotions and being self-aware means understanding your wants, needs, limitations, and strengths. Self-awareness at an early age can benefit early school success. When children can better control themselves, they have an easier time listening to teachers and school staff. Self-awareness is critical for emotional connections.

Children can achieve social success by improving emotional connections. Emotional connections can be built upon the ability to understand and control one's emotions. This way, children are more likely to respond appropriately. Self-awareness guides children to understand the emotions of others and therefore improves communication between themselves and others.

Children 4 years and older can be aware of their psychological selves. Self-understanding is created and influences moral development, self-regulation, and self-control. If a child is able to identify emotions within themselves, they are going to be more successful when transitioning to kindergarten.

Self-management means being able to control behaviors and emotions. Self-management helps children persevere through difficult tasks and situations. Self-management expands in children at a young age. Self-management skills are the foundation for recognizing emotion and adapting our actions accordingly. It's important for children to take part in experiences that challenge them to regulate and manage their emotions. These children are typically cooperative and competent.

Self-management can be promoted through stakeholders in a child's education. The teacher can guide a student through a rough math question, allowing them to get frustrated. A parent can help a child calm down and make a decision rather than throwing a tantrum and yelling. Allowing children to express themselves gives them opportunities to learn more about themselves and their emotions.

Social awareness is critical for social success. Social success has a severe impact on a student's academic success. Social awareness means being aware of the emotions and feelings of those around us. Theory of mind understands how different moods, motivations, levels of knowledge, and beliefs affect our behavior, as well as those surrounding us. Perspective-taking is complemented by the theory of mind.

Perspective-taking means we can relate to others. We can empathize with them and have a better understanding of their point of view. Empathy takes place when we under-stand and recognize the emotions of others. Emotional and academic success are based upon good empathy skills. Because social awareness is critical for empathy, students should develop social awareness at a young age. Studies suggest that when students have stronger perspective-taking skills, they are more liked by their peers and more successful in all of their relationships.

Relationship skills are a determinant of children's acad-emic success. Developing relationship skills allows students to create positive social relationships. These positive rela-tionships can help the child work together with others and better handle conflict. Programs that include teaching social skills, guidance, and opportunities to practice will improve positive relationships with peers, friendship, and acceptance.

When children develop social-emotional skills early on in

life, they are generally more trusting, confident, empathetic, communicative, competent, and inquisitive. They are typically more successful in relationships due to effective communication skills and the ability to avoid and defuse conflict. These students are successful in the classroom and are more engaged and successful than their peers.

Responsible decision-making is when children have learned to make positive choices about their social and personal behavior. Programs that increase responsible decision-making will include a focus on perceptive thinking, reflection, self-direction, problem-solving, and motivation skills. When in social situations or making decisions, it's proven that students need problem-solving skills. Responsible decision-making means acting appropriately, both in and out of school.

EQ VS. IQ

It's been said that a person has multiple intelligences that range across a spectrum and is different from everyone else. Because of the vast types of knowledge among people, how can we only measure how "smart" a child is one way?

Emotional intelligence (EQ) focuses on identifying emotions, understanding how others feel, self-control, empathy, healthy emotional communication, and improved relation to others. Cognitive intelligence (IQ) is measured by knowing, thinking, remembering, problem-solving, and judging.

EQ and IQ are both important for a student's success in school. EQ allows the student to be socially successful and create friendships and healthy relationships. IQ allows the student to make good grades and excel academically. With standardized testing, the child's IQ is being tested. Interestingly, studies now suggest that EQ may be more beneficial than IQ for predicting a students' success.

The school does a great job of building a student's IQ. However, it would be doing an even better job if the school focused on the EQ of students. It's best if EQ is developed in the earlier years, so implementing some sort of storytelling during school hours will allow the children to see and feel various emotions. With storytelling, kids can better relate to situations and handle emotions and events more appropriately.

SEL AND EQUITY IN SCHOOLS

SEL can create just, caring, healthy, and inclusive communities that help all students reach their full potential. Implementing SEL creates an equitable learning environment. In this environment, both students and adults feel valued, affirmed, and important. They feel as though their identities, talents, interests, opinions, and backgrounds are respected and supported.

In the education system, SEL helps schools promote:

- Understanding.
- Anti-racism and ongoing reflection of racism.
- Building intercultural relationships and communication.
- Adult-student relationships to improve overall equity.

It's important for schools to include SEL in programs and curriculum because it can transform a child's experience. With equity, schools can improve educational opportunities and outcomes for all students, regardless of any characteristics or situations they experience.

SEL can be used in school programs to recognize diverse backgrounds and cultures. SEL focuses on the acceptance of all backgrounds and diversities rather than conforming students to a dominant culture. Schools can improve SEL by creating events and programs directed toward community needs and cultural acceptance. It's important to recognize that SEL is for all students systematically, not just for individual students.

SEL means creating an inclusive environment for all involved. SEL is beneficial for improving bad behaviors and mental health, but it can be much more beneficial when creating a framework that includes all areas of schooling. When schools create an overall process to promote EQ and SEL, they can be the most successful when focusing on all parts of a child's life.

In the classroom, SEL can improve competencies and

skills that help students be successful in school. These children go on to contribute more to their careers, schools, relationships, families, and communities. SEL programs are successful when they give the children more opportunities for their education. SEL gives children a decision in their way of learning. They are able to think more on their own and view all others as equal at a young age.

SEL supports the participation of adults to improve equity. SEL programs allow adults to promote equity by addressing the impact of individual racism, oppression, and discrimination on students. Adults can support their children and encourage them to find friends of all races. They can also set a good example for children to be accepting of others. Adults can have an influence over a child's life, so showing others inclusivity teaches the child that accepting others is important.

In order to have a beneficial SEL program, a school must include families, communities, and students in social and emotional development. Including all people involved in a child's life ensures that they are exposed to SEL at all times. The child not only learns SEL, but they learn how SEL applies in various situations. Schools should develop SEL programs that are influenced by the thoughts and opinions of students, community members, and families.

CREATING A SEL PROGRAM

Teachers have a wonderful opportunity to mold what happens in their classroom. Creating an SEL program for your students gives them motivation, tools for success, and a strong education. One way to improve SEL in the classroom is to teach direct lessons about SEL. You can create lessons and plans that are structured around how to be more socially and emotionally intelligent. Some lesson topics include making friends, working in a group, dealing with stress, making decisions, and resolving conflict.

These lessons can include positive human development overall, especially in areas that aren't specifically related to education, such as citizenship and health. SEL content can focus on preventing bad behavior, including bullying, substance use, and violence. Creating a lesson revolving around SEL can teach students to avoid problematic behavior such as bullying, drug addiction, or violence.

Another way you can incorporate SEL in the classroom is by integrating SEL content with the academic curriculum. Some teachers use a core academic subject in order to teach social and emotional skills. When an SEL program is integrated with academics, then it ensures that the core content is being covered and developing social and emotional skills. For example, if you and your students are reading a story, you could have them stop for a moment and write down how they think that character is feeling. This teaches students reading and metaphors while also showing them the importance of human emotion.

Teachers can also use their instructional practices to incorporate SEL in the classroom. Some of these classroom-based programs can focus on the process of teaching children, the process of students learning, and creating a positive environment. Using teacher instructional practices to expand your SEL knowledge in the classroom, you are focusing mainly on making a positive learning experience through different methods and routines. Some of these practices include praise, encouragement, and support.

Programs can use more than one way of delivering SEL knowledge to the students. Programs are specifically customizable to the environment, students, teachers, school, and more. You can use multiple aspects of SEL when creating a program for your students. Perform a needs assessment based on age, academics, community, and current issues. Be prepared to connect current events with your SEL content. This makes your program feel more real to students.

A lot of SEL programs take place through classroom-based lessons. These lessons are usually given during the school day and at a specific time. Aspects of SEL are woven into academic lessons because a lot of teachers have to squeeze a certain amount of information into the school day or year. Many teachers don't have time to make out a program specific for SEL. That's why it's the most common to include SEL in your daily learning.

Some SEL programs are schoolwide. Schoolwide SEL programs promote collaboration and teamwork between different grade levels, classrooms, and students. This can be seen in morning meetings, pep rallies, and clubs and groups. The drama club would be an example of a schoolwide SEL program. SEL programs that are schoolwide are the most successful when they encourage engagement between students through non-teaching practices.

SEL programs that include parents are also very successful, and they promote and reinforce SEL. An SEL program includes the parents when it requires activities or assignments that need to involve the family. This could be a family project. Schools could offer SEL workshops with tips and advice for parents about social and emotional learning.

An SEL program is beneficial when it includes the community. A successful SEL program can reach the community if it provides students with opportunities for long-term relationships, involvement with the community, and personal contacts. When the student can work together with the community successfully, then they are showing positive outcomes from the SEL program.

PROGRAM EFFECTIVENESS

Once you've created and implemented your program, you must decide whether it is successful or not. There are many different aspects of a successful program. Many characteristics and attributes of successful programs can be found through students or teachers. In order to ensure you have created an effective program, give the students the opportunity to practice.

When you have created a program, you are aiming to teach them something new and structuring their learning material so they can learn it easier. Once you have presented the new program to the children, give them time to work with the information. Giving them the information and then asking them to practice and work with it allows them to deal with and store the information independently.

When you deliver material, it lands in your students' short-term memory. When you give them the opportunity to practice and come to terms with the new information, it will then be transferred to the long-term memory. You'll never be able to transfer every bit of information into his students' long-term memory. However, the goal is to get across the most important parts of your lesson.

Practice also improves social and emotional skills. Practice is important, especially when it is outside of the academic setting. This is when the outcome of practice is the most powerful. Programs are the most successful when they provide learning opportunities beyond or during classroom time. When children are allowed to practice material on their own, they get a better grasp of the information. They are allowed to get personal with the information and make connections to old information, making it easier to understand. Practice during and after classroom time is going to give you the most success.

During class, you can use practice such as role-play and guided self-management advice. Once out of the classroom, you want students to be able to apply aspects of social and emotional learning to real-life circumstances, like using problem-solving skills or self-calming techniques during conflicts. The program is successful when your student is able to take the information they have learned in class and apply it to their real-life without the assistance of other adults.

A program is successful when students leave with more knowledge than they had when they came. A great program can motivate and excite the child to use that information in real life. Your program should benefit the students' entire life, inside and out of school.

You can determine the success of your SEL program based on your and your student's experience. If you cannot deliver all of the information you want to in your SEL program, but you and the students are both happy with your outcomes, then the SEL program could be considered successful.

Setting goals as a classroom can also determine the success of an SEL program. Creating goals with students allows you both to agree on what is going to be needed to pass. If you have met your goal, then your SEL program is successful. In order to determine if you've met your goal, you have to perform an assessment.

ASSESSMENT

Assessments give you an idea of your student's knowledge at a given time. You can perform assessments before, during, and after creating your program. There are four main types of assessments: diagnostic, formative, interim, and summative.

Diagnostic assessments are done before creating the program in order to see what is needed and how to structure the program. Formative assessments are done during the program to track progress and see if there need to be any changes done to the strategy and delivery. Interim assessments are done to determine the progress of the entire school, team, group, or student body. Summative assessments are done in order to see how the program can improve for the next time.

It's important that diagnostic assessments are done in the pre-planning stages, so you have an accurate assessment of current knowledge. You need to know what your students already know, so you can build new information off of that old information, and you can better structure your assessment.

Formative assessments are commonly given in the middle of the program. This is used to understand how the students are understanding and progressing. Formative assessments are beneficial for allowing you to make any changes that are needed, so you can have better outcomes.

Interim assessments determined the knowledge of the

entire group and are used to compare to smaller groups of students. Having a broad idea of what an entire group knows, you can better select your group and see how well they know it compared to their peers. Interim assessments allow you to see if there are parts of a group that aren't doing as well as the whole. This could show problems in delivery, inclusion, environment, and much more.

A benchmark assessment is used to measure the entire progress of a large group of students. The benchmark assessment is beneficial for showing how well the students have done altogether.

A summative assessment occurs at the end of a lesson or checkpoint. The summative assessment is beneficial for determining if the program was successful or not or if the goal was reached or not.

Assessments help teachers decide what to teach, how to teach it, and how well they taught it in the end. Assessments are also beneficial for determining the strengths and weaknesses of each student. Once a teacher has this information, they can use it to alter their program. With an assessment, you can help develop your students, track student performance, and improve successful student learning.

An important part of an assessment also includes some sort of option for feedback. Feedback is important for helping you decide how you can make the program better for next time. Feedback gives you a perspective that you cannot see as the creator. You can gather feedback from your students by a survey, having them draw a picture of how well you did, writing you an essay, or more.

POTENTIAL PITFALLS

As with any program implementation, there can be pitfalls and blindspots we encounter. Even with the best intentions, no program will be fool-proof on the first try. The student body and their needs are always changing. Programs and curriculum should change with them. Although needs are constantly changing, there are still some mistakes that are made with trying to implement SEL for improving educational equity.

When trying to implement SEL, it can be hard to see situations that we have never been in before. When dealing with multiple diverse cultures, races, and backgrounds, one group of people will not be able to grasp all of the problems and situations they face. This deficit mindset could leave opportunities for failure or leave some students out.

Another potential issue of SEL programs could be having an over-emphasis on self-regulation and self-management instead of the development of the human mind. Schools would rather students listen and follow directions instead of speak out and voice their opinions. When students can take an involved approach in their learning, they feel more comfortable contributing new ideas and then participating in their education plan. Schools see children as being defiant or non-compliant when resisting practices and structures that they experience as threatening rather than allowing them to shift their content plan.

One potential problem of SEL programs is setting them to have colorblind principles. These programs can teach children to "see no color." We don't want a colorblind world. Instead, SEL programs should teach children to see the other colors, races, backgrounds, cultures, and more and celebrate and accept them. The point isn't to get children to erase their culture to blend in; it is to create a more understanding and accepting group of people. SEL programs should normalize seeing the different races and cultures and viewing different experiences through the lens of power, culture, and race.

When implementing SEL, it can be easy to act on our unconscious stereotypes and biases. We can miss opportunities to be better because of preconceived notions. It's important for adults, school administrators, and all stakeholders to avoid letting previous experiences and interests impact SEL program decisions. In this situation, it's important to have a vastly diverse group making these SEL programs. That way, there are more opinions and perceptions going into the program. There's less of a chance of a bias or deficits slipping through.

One more pitfall of some SEL programs is benefitting SEL among students but not helping where it's actually needed. When creating an SEL program, there should be an analysis of the problems being faced. Without accurately researching what is needed, making an SEL program could leave you with a beneficial but useless program. SEL programs can be beneficial when focusing on helping students gain skills and resources that they don't have otherwise. Creating an after-school program for math tutoring improves math scores but won't be very beneficial if the majority of the class is struggling with reading.

IMPROVING SEL WITH STUDENTS

SEL programs do not have to be just school or county-wide. SEL can be implemented and taught in all parts of the students' lives. Teachers have a strong impact on improving SEL just in their classrooms. Teachers can act as a model for their students to be more socially and emotionally intelligent. Teachers can use their actions and attitudes to show students the proper ways of being socially and emotionally intelligent.

Due to the high importance of academic marks and testing scores, teachers have less of an opportunity to teach students the "soft" skills, such as those that allow students to connect with others. It can also be intimidating for teachers to add yet another responsibility to their plate by agreeing to implement SEL principles. However, SEL integration is almost guaranteed to improve the performance, attitudes, and outcomes of students. Teachers can create SEL programs and initiatives by:

- Defining goals for the class, including expectations for behavior.

- Explaining what the goals are and what the behavior should look like.
- Creating planning cycles and assessments to re-evaluate SEL success regularly.
- Aligning your classroom goals with school goals.
- Using integrated instruction and modeling.
- Providing opportunities to practice SEL skills.
- Establishing regular check-ins to measure student's mental health and emotional connectivity, and ability.
- Connecting and working with seasoned SEL professionals.

Some great ways you can use SEL in your educational activities are listed below.

1. Use journal writing. You can have the student write anything they want, or you can give them a prompt. For example: write one paragraph about what you did this weekend. Let's say you meet a new person. What would you say to them? How would you describe yourself to someone else? This can be done weekly, daily, or even monthly.
2. Use stories and characters. Read a story aloud and have the children take turns reading. Ask them how the characters felt in certain parts of the play. You could make it fun and have the children read as though they are portraying the

character. The students have fun because they feel they're being silly, but they're actually trying to understand how the character feels and how to portray that. This gives them an SEL opportunity to learn and practice their skills.

3. Make a connection through greetings. Children, just like adults, need connection. Spending just a few seconds to say hey and high-five with each child as they walk in your classroom can establish a connection that they can keep with them throughout the class.

4. Have class meetings. During these meetings, you could go over what you're going to learn for that day/week. You could have them on Fridays and cover everything you learned for the week. Ask the students what they liked the most and why they liked it. This also gives the students the opportunity to participate in class. You can all identify problems you might be having and work to fix them together.

5. Use art activities. Have children cut up old magazines and create self-collages. Tell them to find pictures and colors that define them. Allowing children to cut, color, paint, etc., let them express themselves.

6. Give responsibilities. When students have a job they have to do, such as line leader or class

librarian, they get a stronger sense of community and self-worth.

7. Give them opportunities to use their problem-solving skills. Instead of solving a problem for them right away, allow them to try and work it out on their own.

8. Use teamwork. Teamwork can build a sense of community, problem-solving skills, critical thinking, and participation.

9. Increase positive self-talk. Teach children to be proud of themselves so they don't have to rely on the approval of others when gauging self-worth. Positive thoughts can improve the child's confidence and social and academic success.

10. Use hands-on crafts. Students can use this time to let out any nervous energy they may have.

11. Encourage reflection. Reflection allows the child to think back on what happened and how it made them feel.

12. Practice mindfulness. Practicing mindfulness as a child teaches them to take a second to control their breathing, focus on one thing at a time, and relax their bodies.

13. Use a calm-down area. This area can be a small bean bag chair in the corner with some books and fidget toys. This allows the student to release any rough emotions they may be struggling with. They can return to the class once they've calmed down.

The area will be a safe space for the children to explore their emotions and work through them, rather than suppressing them.

14. Encourage kindness. Being kind to one another is one of the best ways to create relationships. Teaching the children kindness and respect will make them more socially successful.

15. Have a weekly check-in. Try to get each student pulled to the side and talked to once a week. See how the child is doing and what you can do to help them if they need it.

You've got the idea of programs you can use to implement SEL into your classroom. Get creative with ways to implement SEL. You can change it up every week or pick a few processes and stick with them. Make sure to find out what your students like, what they need, and what they want.

If you are looking to quick-start SEL in your classroom, we have a 5-day challenge for free at the end of this book!

COLLEGE AND CAREER

As studies progress, pressure can be put on colleges to include social intelligence as factors when regarding admission, grades, and graduation. SEL can improve success in students' lives, whether they choose college, career, or any other path they decide. SEL is extremely beneficial when a student transitions to college. Not only will the students have to make new friendships and relationships, but they are typically immersed in a large group of people they've never met before. This can cause stress in children who aren't very socially and emotionally intelligent. However, when children have high SEL skills, they are able to navigate the crowd and create beneficial and supportive relationships.

College also requires SEL because it is extremely stressful, especially for freshmen making one of the biggest transitions in their lives. Having SEL skills allows students to be able to control their emotions and complete their work without being controlled by their stress. Being able to better manage their emotions is going to help their academic and social performance.

Social performance is beneficial in college because it can create networking and job opportunities. Meeting and conversing with more people allows students to meet cultures and races they hadn't met before. This gives them more exposure to other mindsets, beliefs, and practices. It also creates opportunities for students to use to improve their chances of getting a job after graduation.

Businesses look for emotional intelligence in their employees. Being emotionally intelligent allows their employees to be more creative and productive. Socially and emotionally intelligent workers can join together to work and solve problems. Group work can increase morale, participation, and productivity. Employers understand the importance of emotional intelligence and aim to choose employees who meet these criteria.

When hiring, companies look for SEL skills because these employees typically respond better to feedback, make better decisions, and are more motivated to align with the company's morals and values. It's also worth mentioning that students with high SEL skills go on to have more successful, long-term careers. SEL-skilled employees also have an easier time problem-solving.

5

UDL AND IMPLEMENTATION

Universal Design for Learning (UDL) is a thought process that aims to give equal opportunities to all students in order to be successful. This approach allows for more flexibility regarding students' access to material, engaging with that material, and showing what they've learned. UDL can benefit every child, but it is especially beneficial for kids with thinking and learning differences.

When you think of the term "universal," you think of a plan that will find one way of teaching that benefits all students. In actuality, UDL is about creating a teaching method that removes barriers to education and learning and aims to give all students an equal opportunity to succeed. UDL is about including flexibility to fit the strengths and needs of children. UDL is beneficial for children diagnosed with learning disorders and those without illness or without a diagnosis.

UDL is important for equity in education because it ensures all students are given equal opportunities to be successful in their education. People encounter UDL every day, even when they don't know it. You can find UDL through automatic doors, accessibility features on technology, and closed captions. While these are designed for people who may need assistance, they benefit all people. UDL allows teachers to use flexibility and aids in teaching where it helps some students and benefits all students. This increases student access to the material.

Dewi (2019) combined research based on UDL in the classroom and teacher/student involvement. Based on research, UDL was shown to have three vital parts for successful program creation: representation, action and expression, and engagement. When using UDL to develop a lesson plan and assessment, it's important to include these principles.

REPRESENTATION

Representation means offering the material in multiple formats. When there are more options for learning, more students can learn successfully. A textbook is a visual way of learning. If you add hands-on activities, videos, and songs, your students will have a better chance of retaining the content. These efforts benefit all students but also allows them to choose the best way of learning for them. This teaches them what they're good at and how they can learn material for the future.

Options for representing the material to students are important for reaching out to every student. Not only will the multiple formats reach students who have disabilities, but it'll also help the students who learn more with multiple ways of interacting with the material. One student may need visual assistance, and this visual assistance could benefit another student who has perfect eyesight.

To improve representation, key information should be perceptible to all students. You can do this by presenting the information in more than one sense (vision, smell, taste, etc.). Another way is making the information malleable by the students who need more assistance. Think of allowing the student to zoom in and out of pictures and turn the volume up or down. Giving students a flexible format for content delivery is beneficial because it allows them to change their lesson aspects. For example, let students:

- Change the size of graphs, images, visual content, tables, etc.
- Alter the brightness or contrast of a photo
- Pick the colors of highlighted information/information on the marker board
- Adjust the volume and playback speed
- Customize the timing and speed of the sound, animation, video, etc.
- Choose fonts
- Vote on the layout of material

Providing more options for comprehending information among students ensures you have given students at least one way of learning that works best for them. Assignments and options for math expressions, symbols, and language can allow students to express themselves in a way that fits them the best. When students can control and choose their education, they're more involved and more successful.

Representation is important because, without it, many children could fall behind in their studies. Even if there is just one lesson that isn't easily accessible to them, all of the information built off of that lesson will be blurred. This lesson could have acted as a foundation for all information after, but now the child will have a harder time building their knowledge. Vocabulary words are a great way to provide strong foundations for students.

Language is different among all children. Some are foreign, others are born in different states, and even slang is different among all families. Having regular vocabulary lessons helps the students understand more of the basics. Providing vocabulary grows the children's minds by allowing them to associate one meaning with a word. This way, everyone in the learning environment is clear on what is needed for success. Clarity among students is important for decreasing frustration among students.

When students feel represented in the classroom, they're going to take more pride in their work. Students who are different, who have disabilities, get frustrated with themselves and their education and feel isolated and alone. When they are given more measures they need to reach a goal, they feel like a bigger part of the classroom.

When you include representation in your curriculum and classroom, children are more likely to be motivated, receptive, and relaxed. This is the perfect state of mind for learning. This shows how teachers can build a strong learning environment. When your students feel a sense of belonging, they're going to create better relationships with the teacher, students, and school. Research can prove that a sense of belonging can lead to academic success.

In a study of 528 educators, 41% reported it to be challenging to ensure their students have a sense of belonging (Blad, 2017). 80% reported how important belonging was, and 49% stated they needed help finding more strategies for increasing feelings of belonging among students (Blad, 2017). You can increase the sense of belonging among your students in lots of fun ways.

1. Start with introductions. Introducing yourself and your students to each other will immediately create relationships and friends. Learn the students' names and faces as soon as you can. One fun way to increase belonging is to have an ice breaker. An ice breaker is a joke or game you play throughout the classroom. Each student can tell a story or say something about themselves to the classroom. This creates a bonding experience between students and teachers. This bit of story told by each student will help everyone remember them and their name.

2. Make the teacher-student relationship a priority. Make sure you have office hours, or you can set meetings. Allow your students to reach out to you and talk about their questions and needs.

3. Cultivate a caring and supportive environment. Show students they should be comfortable in their learning environment. This makes them more impressionable and welcoming to the idea of change. Showcase student strengths.

4. Be welcoming with your students' emotions and needs. If they come to you with problems, see if they can be solved by allowing more representation in the classroom. Maybe a child is shy, and they have trouble participating in group discussions. Instead, you could have them journal

their thoughts and hand them to you. This could be their participation grade.

5. Set your expectations and standards. When students are clear on what they need to be successful, they will know the tools they require to get there. Then the students will be able to come to you if they need help getting access to something.

6. Show interest in your students. When they feel heard, they feel like they belong. Allow the children a moment to talk about themselves, their day, or their week. Ask them questions to learn more about them. Creating a stronger relationship is going to allow you to see problems the student might be having, even if they don't recognize it themselves.

7. Create a sense of community in your classroom. Ask your students to create some ground rules for the classroom. Encourage your students to speak out. You all can work together to create an inclusive educational environment!

When students feel represented, they are more motivated to act and express themselves.

ACTION AND EXPRESSION

Action and expression include opportunities for students to interact with the content in more than one way and show what they retained. Instead of a typical pencil-paper test, students could have the opportunity to do an oral report or a group project. Providing options for action and expression is important because not all students will act and express themselves the same way.

Make sure that your students have some freedom in choosing the timing, speed, rate, and range of motion required for instructions. Give the children options for acting and expressing themselves in their lesson. Giving students more control over their emotions towards learning can help them gain more motivation for engagement.

Many children have disabilities and differences in motor skills. Instead of having children write with pencil and paper, allow them to use a computer, or vice versa. You can provide an adapted keyboard or larger pencils with grips for children who need or want them. This stems from UDL because the adapted keyboards may be directed for a few, but they can be beneficial for all.

Allow students access to the technologies and tools they need for action and expression. Instructional content should not include barriers that prevent children from getting access to the extra tools they need. You can provide access to extra tools without removing the challenge from the learning lesson.

Improving accessibility is not about making it easier for students to pass their assignments; it's about giving them the same opportunities as other children when it comes to academic success. If a student has poor attention skills, you don't want to just give them good grades because they have it harder than other students. You should move them closer up front, see about getting therapy for the child if they're too distracted, and more. You need to leave the challenges in learning, so children are forced to think hard and get better.

You can include more activities to allow the children to show action and expression. These opportunities can be:

- Giving options for student response.
- Allowing more than one option when students are showing their knowledge
- Use an assessment based on the format of each student's work
- Encourage use of various tools for students to use when expressing their feelings

When you increase opportunities for students to act and express, you are improving engagement.

ENGAGEMENT

Engagement encourages looking for ways to motivate students. This means including assignments that are relative to the students' lives and can gain their attention. Making games that allow skill-building and allowing movement around the room can help students engage in their material.

Students learn differently in the way they engage with the material and their motivations to learn. Some children engage the best with visual material, while others need auditory in addition to visual. Some have internal motivators, and some have external motivators. Children's learning behaviors are affected by culture, subjectivity, personal relevance, neurology, background knowledge, and much more. Providing multiple ways for students to engage with the material ensures that all students are given the same opportunity to learn the content.

When you are trying to increase engagement, be sure to focus on the students' interests. Irrelevant information can go unprocessed and unnoticed. Because of this, teachers can have a hard time getting the students to listen to the material continuously. Target your student's interests when looking to improve engagement. Engagement can also improve by encouraging individual choice in class.

Giving the student more choices in their learning allows for a deeper connection. Individual choice fosters self-determination and pride in their accomplishments. You can allow your students to have a choice by:

- How they will be rewarded for a challenge
- Where/when to cover certain material
- How to cover material
- What is going to be used for the lesson
- What they will physically do

These are just a few of the ways that students can have their own choices in class. It's important to include the choices of surrounding adults and the community to improve engagement. Since there are many people that affect a child's education, it's important for them to engage in the students' learning as well. Improving engagement among support systems improves engagement for children. This, overall, improves the child's performance.

Engagement can be held back by threats and distractions. In order to make a safe space for learners, teachers have to reduce threats and distractions. These situations can cloud the learning environment and affect the transfer of the content. You can create a safe space for students to learn in many ways. You just have to get creative.

- Promote a supportive and accepting climate for your classroom
- Use routines and calendars/charts/graphics to show the predictability of the class and material. For example, have a calendar on the board of what you're going to be covering in class that day or week.
- Give enough notice so students can prepare for changes in schedules and activities.
- Keep an eye on the sensory stimulation. This can include background noise, visual, audio, or the number of items presented at one time. If you're playing a video while talking to another teacher

and there are cars honking outside, chances are high the student isn't going to be able to fully listen.

- Have a classroom-wide discussion and include all students. Call on the students who haven't added anything to the discussion and ask them what they think.

You can also improve engagement if you include value, authenticity, and relevance. When information is valuable and relevant to a student's needs and wants, they want to listen. They are going to have an easier time connecting with the material. It should also be aligned with instructional goals to ensure academic success.

Vary your sources of information and activities. This keeps your material socially relevant, age-appropriate, culturally relevant, and personalized to students' needs. After finding information, design your activities so that the outcomes of learning are clear and authentic. The tasks should promote participation, experimentation, and exploration. These thought-provoking tasks open the child's mind up to learning more about themselves. Activities that require imagination to solve problems will force the children to think outside the box.

All children are different when it comes to self-regulation. Some can hold their attention long enough to finish a task when motivated to do so. Other students may not be able to. Building the idea of self-regulation and self-determination in students will allow all to have the same chances of finishing a task attentively. To help in the classroom, allow improved accessibility options to students who have less self-regulation and motivation.

Some students need constant reminders of the goal or reward at the end. This acts as their motivation for finishing a project. Others may need help remembering the goal and the steps to achieve that goal. The students should be reminded of the goal or reward when they are facing distractions. You can do this by:

- Having the student recite the goal weekly.
- Putting the goal in multiple areas that the student will see (on the board, on their test, etc.).
- Breaking down large goals into smaller short-term objectives. This makes your students feel like it's more attainable.

Learners need to be challenged in order to be successful. They just need to be challenged in different ways than one another. Vary resources and needs to challenge the student and improve their motivation. You can also increase motivation and engagement by allowing flexibility when choosing what tools to use when completing the challenge. Let them also have a say in what is successful. When they are clear on what it takes to succeed, and they decide how they can succeed, they have better chances of doing well.

In order to promote engagement, learners need a

supportive community and collaboration. Collaboration and community create mentorship among peers. Peers will be able to count on each other to reach a goal. They will be able to collaborate creatively. Flexible grouping can improve differentiation and creates multiple roles. Groups allow different options to grow important skills. To promote group work:

- Create clear roles, goals, and responsibilities
- Make cooperative learning groups
- Increase schoolwide programs that promote positive behavior and improve different supports, interests, and objectives
- Allow a channel for students to talk to each other and work together
- Create communities of like-minded children with similar activities or interests.
- Clarify expectations

One fun way to use UDL in the classroom is by allowing students to show their knowledge in different ways. You could have them draw a picture or make a video about a lesson you just gave. You can always give them the option for an essay or test if that's what they feel comfortable doing. Overall, UDL will improve the learners' entire learning process. Studies show a positive association between UDL and increased learning.

One researcher found that giving subject matter in more than one way increased student interest in learning and increased their access to lecture material (Dewi, 2019). Across multiple studies, UDL showed increased learning among students (Dewi, 2019). When a research group used video games and books, instead of textbooks, for learning, students were more likely to retain more knowledge and have better access to the content (Dewi, 201). When teachers were providing more options for the students to learn, students were more interested and involved.

UDL combined with technology creates a vast amount of opportunities for students. A child could be given the option to listen to a video lecture or do some of their own research on a computer. A student could use a T-93 calculator, and another uses an iPad for help with math.

6

STRATEGIES AND PLANS

No two students are exactly alike, and that's why equity in the classroom is important. Teachers should pride themselves in having an equitable classroom because they are giving their students an advantage for success. Having an equitable classroom is something important to build because it can benefit both you and the students.

Teachers and students together bring different information, such as:

- Traumas
- Biases
- Stereotypes
- Identities
- Previous experiences

- Assumptions
- Cultures
- Backgrounds

When teachers and students work together, they can create an environment that's rich enough for the students to grow and flourish. In all students, there is one class that a student will remember more than the others. Whether it was a good class, a bad class, or a good or bad teacher, there are experiences that will stand out to that student for their lifetime.

Having SEL in the classroom will teach students important skills that can improve their performance in other classes and in life. When you combine UDL with SEL, you can create an unstoppable criterion that's sure to cultivate learning in your students. SEL is what the lesson contains or consists of. UDL is how the material is delivered.

Combining UDL with SEL means creating lessons, plans, or programs that are SEL-related and given with UDL in mind. There are some activities and situations where UDL and SEL go hand-in-hand. One activity can cover both models and even include an academic lesson.

However, there will be times when you do not have time to create three separate lesson plans and then combine them together. Teachers already work much more time than they're paid, plus it can be exhausting to try and think of all of these lesson plans at once.

There are techniques, tips, and tricks you can use when

aiming to improve UDL and SEL in your classroom. For starters, you can attend any special speeches or presentations regarding UDL and SEL. Most schools will allow teachers a "professional day" where the teacher can do something education-related in order to help their students.

You can also meet with other teachers and experts in your field. You can look on LinkedIn and find others who are experienced in what you need and look for a mentor. A mentor is someone you will be able to reach out to in time of need and doubt. A mentor could also be someone in your school or in another school district.

You may be able to keep UDL consistent throughout the school year. This means you can make arrangements at the beginning of your year to improve choices for students throughout class time. You can change all videos on your computer and lessons to use captions (or having the ability to turn them on/off). You could arrange for laptops or iPads to be able to be checked out by students when needed.

Some teachers have access to other teachers that have previously taught your subject or class. Reach out to these teachers and see if they have any assignments or ideas they can share with you.

The research will also help you in improving UDL and SEL in the classroom. The body of research on education is consistently growing, and it's important to stay up to date on new theories of education and learning.

Keep your notes and your plans organized. It can be

daunting to look at everything written down at once. Make yourself notes. Write down everything you want to achieve in your classroom. For each item, write down two actions you and your students can take to reach that goal. Those actions can then be broken down into more actions when needed.

Creating this plan is going to allow you to break down what you want and need to do. Include notes and research on any theories you specifically want to discuss in class, such as self-discipline and making good decisions when in distress.

Look at the year ahead and see what you can include to help your students. Do they have a big end-of-year test? Teach them coping anxiety mechanisms and test-taking skills. Every student tests differently; use UDL to teach them how they should take a test. This can remove test anxiety so their scores can be better.

Talking to your students is a great way to determine what you want and need from your class. Getting their input shows them you think their opinion is important, and you want to work with them to be successful.

Share your power with your students. Letting them make decisions for you can release some pressure from you, and it can improve their motivation and engagement. When you remove the superiority from the teacher and make them more of a guide than a disciplinary, students are going to feel a stronger connection with that teacher.

Take advantage of informal learning lessons. Being in school all day, every day is exhausting for students and teachers. Informal learning takes place in a casual manner. You may be able to do more than you would in a traditional classroom, such as taking a walk or moving around in the gym. Informal learning also shows students you're passionate about reaching all students.

Be creative and persuasive with the administration. If your students are stressed out, take them to the gym and allow them to answer review questions. If they get one right, they can either walk a lap, shoot a basketball, or do some jumping jacks for a bonus point on the test. This gives the student opportunities to earn points for their test, retain information from the review, and let out energy that you all have.

When working with your students, the administration may be a problem because of the strict restrictions on teachers. Being persuasive with the administration means trying to come to an agreement. If the administration has the gym booked for that day, take the students outside instead or reschedule for another day.

Arrange for field trips when possible. Field trips are a great way to make students more excited about learning. They get a "break" from school while still being able to learn. They get real-life and hands-on experience regarding what they're learning in class.

Reach out to the community for ideas and options. You

could reach out to the fire department and ask them for a demonstration on how to put out a fire, then let the children ask the firemen questions. You can ask local clubs, groups, and businesses if they offer any volunteer opportunities or events. Allow your students the option to participate in an outside event or volunteer instead of submitting homework one day.

Have a career day and/or college day. Have local businesses and experts come to the school and set up tables for the students to visit and ask any questions regarding work or college. This provides students with a glimpse of their future and what their life could look like after school. They may also find their passion at an early age and therefore have more time to pursue their life goals.

Have two formats for a test. One version could be all true/false, and another version could be multiple choice. Both tests contain the same information, but students are able to choose the format of their test.

Watch out for students cheating. Cheating can be a sign that a student needs help. Many times, cheating is severely punished but not necessarily questioned about why it happened. Maybe the student couldn't study because their mother was sick in the hospital. One student may not have been able to grasp a part of the lesson and is looking to another student for help. It could even be the fact that the student was lazy and simply didn't study. Regardless of cheating, ask yourself (and the student) why they felt the need to cheat. Finding out the reason behind cheating can be very informational.

TECHNOLOGY AND EDUCATION

Using technology is a great way to improve UDL and SEL. Technology allows students a leg up in learning. You can find that many public schools today offer, for every five students, at least one computer. One of the biggest challenges facing education today is the inability of all students to access WiFi and the Internet outside of school. Many kids in remote and rural areas don't have access to the Internet and online classes or education. Even standardized testing is gradually switching to computer tests.

Unequal use of the Internet causes students to be left behind when they need extra research. When all students do not have access to the Internet outside of the classroom, you cannot give them an assignment that requires internet access. In order to use technology for equity, you could allow that student to use the computer outside of class times. You could also allow them to complete the assignment another way.

Many education experts suggest using new technologies in school to reach more diverse student populations. Those who speak a foreign language could use the computer for assistance in English. You could switch the language on the computer to Spanish, long enough for them to understand the assignment. Then they can complete the assignment in English.

Technology can improve equity in education by:

- Using each student's strengths and weaknesses.
- Finding the users' motivations and interests.
- Emphasizing personal preferences.
- Increasing accessibility to content.
- Providing another way for students to interact with the material.
- Using each student's own learning pace.

Using technology for these benefits can lead to personalized learning. Personalized learning means that the content and delivery are arranged around the student and their needs and wants.

Personalized learning includes having a learner profile. A learner profile is an area of information on the student. This profile can have examples of their work, notes on previous grades or projects, preferences, goals, strengths, weaknesses, progress, and more. This learner profile is customized to each student to show more information about the way they learn.

Students should be motivated to set and achieve their own academic goals. When children want to do well in school, they are typically more academically successful. Their goals can be as small as finishing a worksheet or as big as making an A for the entire year. Encourage students to set goals and feel proud of themselves when they achieve them.

Including competency-based progression in personalized learning allows students to show what they've learned about a topic instead of how long they take to learn it. Having a flexible progression program allows all students to show their knowledge in ways that best suit them.

Lastly, personalized learning creates flexible learning environments that structure and support student goals. When students pick goals, they need help achieving them, or they could become discouraged and have high levels of self-doubt.

Technology can support personalized learning when schools allow students to take tablets and computers home or bring their devices to school. Student information systems and learning management systems can be used for assignments, communications, schedules, and student progress. In this situation, technology allows students to complete an assignment how they want, and when they can and turn it all into the same place. This keeps it organized and beneficial for personalized learning.

Educational applications and software are more adaptive by using algorithms and technology to understand students' knowledge, feelings and emotional state, and progress.

DIGITAL DISTRACTIONS

When dealing with technology, digital distractions can be a big problem. Digital distractions act as a barrier between a student and their education. Even adults are bad about frequently checking their phones during work, social, or class environments. Notifications and being in constant communication with others can keep us distracted while using technology. Digital distractions can break your concentration, slow your reading, and negatively impact your studying habits.

Digital distractions can be especially tough for students with learning disabilities. People who are frustrated with their work, confused, or have diagnosed learning disabilities are going to find it easier to wander away from their task.

Using technology can be great for learning. You can do things to prevent or minimize digital distractions to enhance learning. One way to decrease digital distractions is to remove as many distractions as you can. Put any technology away when you are doing class and study time that doesn't require the computer. Have students put away their electronics in their backpacks or lockers when they aren't being used for class.

Have the devices put on silent mode or turn off the notifications so they won't distract you during teaching times. While using the device, make sure there aren't any other apps or websites open that you don't need at the time.

Letting students use headphones can help them focus on

the task at hand. You can also teach students to catch themselves when they start to lose interest. They could be tired, bored, frustrated, confused, annoyed, and more. Teach them to recognize when they're feeling this way, so they know when to stop and focus.

Another way to avoid distractions is motivating and inspiring your students to complete their assignments and tasks to achieve their goals. When they're more inspired and motivated to work, they are less likely to be distracted. This can allow them to laser focus on their assignment.

You can motivate and inspire students by reminding them of the goal. You can have the children be reminded of their goals by having them write a letter to their future selves. Tell the student what they would say to themselves three months from now if they've reached their goal.

Remind children of the reasons why they are trying to reach their goal. At one point, they were probably excited to achieve their goal. You have to remind them of their reasons so they can get excited again and want to work harder.

Use distractions as rewards. Allow students 10 minutes at the end of every class to play a game, listen to music, perform research, etc. The students can use this time as motivation to focus on and finish their lesson.

Making a list also allows students to see what needs to be done so they can focus on the next task. One stone in Spanish one area of the assignment they may jump to games because they don't want to move ahead. However, if they have a list of the assignments, they will know there's more coming next.

Allow the students an opportunity to track their progress. Just like with the list, students will be able to see how much longer they have left. This can allow them to focus on their assignment instead of counting down the minutes until they can play their game.

You can use some computer settings in order to decrease distractions. You can turn off sounds and notifications. You can lock any music or game apps with a password. That way, students won't be able to play a game app instead of their assignment. Preventing distractions can guide the student through finishing their task.

Using full-screen mode can hide parts of the computer that can distract the student. In some circumstances, you can allow the student to change the settings, so they don't get distracted. They can control the volume, brightness, arrangement of tabs, windows, apps, etc.

Structure study and technology time, so students don't get bored and let their minds disappear from the lesson. Students will have a better time staying focused when there's a set amount of time for each part of their lesson. Look for distractions that students might have. This could be new clothes or shoes, other students, other classes, outside noise, etc.

BUILDING EQUITY

It can be daunting to want to change your class, let alone the entire school. However, once you've changed your class, you will have the experience and confidence to change the school. Change, however, doesn't happen overnight. It takes time, and if you want it done correctly, you must cultivate supporters around you. You have to teach the next genera-tion how important equity is so they can uphold the values after we are gone. The point is to leave the school in a better place than when we were there.

Improving equity in schools allows us to create leaders who will create a more passionate and supportive future for everyone. Some students can easily find their passion during their school years. These children are usually ambitious in getting what they want. These students can be shown their passion through equity.

Equity allows teachers to create leaders. Students who are more well-rounded and have access to more opportuni-ties will gain experience that helps them in the future. There are natural-born leaders, but there are also man-made lead-ers. If the right child is shown their strengths at an early age, they're going to be more confident in leading themselves and their peers.

Teachers should build up students to transform the future, rather than just prepare for it. Showing students how important equity is can allow them to carry those values for the rest of their lives. The more generations of students who experience equity, the more it will become normal practice in schools everywhere.

The future lies in the hands of our children now. We must teach them to be leaders so they can work to create equity even when schools and administrators aren't able to. One student could offer a copy of their notes to another student that has eyesight trouble. Another could offer to help a student with math during recess because they're having trouble understanding a new concept. When given the opportunity, students can help each other and show them what it's like to be a leader.

Teaching the students to be self-sufficient allows them to take the concept of equity through their years of schooling and pass it onto the next generation. When all people understand the importance of equity, we can all work together to make the change.

In order to prepare children to change their future:

- Teach students to have a responsibility when handling freedom. Tell the students you're going to step into the hall for five minutes and tell them not to raise their voices. If they're not loud for those five minutes, you could reward them with no homework for that day or bonus points. This way, children are sure to understand that they're more likely to get more responsibilities when they can handle freedom responsibly.
- Instill a community-oriented mindset. When

students focus on the whole rather than the parts, they will make decisions that are going to best for the most people involved. Children will learn that their actions have consequences, and caring for other people will help humanity. Children should learn that when they work together, they can create some real positive changes.

- Encourage the children to have an open mind. They are going to encounter a lot of situations and instances in their life where they have never seen something before. It can be common to be angry, confused, or scared of the new experience. Preparing children for these diverse interactions will better protect them from shock and misplaced emotions.

- Show children they can help others without taking from themselves. Sometimes children, and even adults, are hesitant to help others due to the chance they could take their support or take success from them. Show children that it's okay to help others and that occasionally going out of their way to help someone can make a big difference.

- Instill a growth mindset. Showing children that they're capable of amazing things can motivate them to work hard. Children can see their true potential when they are taking a growth mindset.

Building equity means making changes now that will lead

to a better future for your school. Building long-term equity means teaching others how important it is and what tools they can use to achieve equity. Children can work together to create equity amongst each other. They can also take these ideas and beliefs with them into further schooling and workplaces.

Not only will children be able to work together when creating equity, but they can also work to create equity for themselves in the future. They are going to be able to better recognize when things aren't equitable and bring it to the attention of others who can help make a change. Showing students the importance, and benefits, of equity, can make them conscious of the problems around them. It will instill a group work ethic, and they can use this to work with others in the professional world.

PROJECT-BASED LEARNING

Children learn better when their material is individualized, important, and relevant. They're also going to have an easier time learning content when they take part in real-world teaching and engagement. Project-based learning (PBL) is a method for teaching where students engage with real-world and meaningful projects to learn more effectively.

PBL is a teaching method that instructors can use to solve real-world problems or answer complex questions. Students are then able to combine their knowledge to show to an audience. They take part in the project, gather their notes and information learned, and compile them into a project to deliver or turn in. After project completion, students have developed their critical thinking skills, creativity, communication skills, and collaboration.

PBL can take anywhere from one week to the entire semester. Students need enough time to gather the information, retain it, then present it. Many times, PBL takes place with bigger projects that involve others in the school or places in the community. When students can work together in PBL, they create creative and contagious energy among other teachers and students.

Every project does not include PBL. Because a teacher assigns a project, it doesn't necessarily mean it's associated with PBL. There are smaller projects, in the sense that the project is over one unit or lesson covered in class that day/week. PBL requires knowledge over multiple areas and using it to solve problems and gain skills and education for the real world.

For example, a shorter project would be creating a presentation over a unit or lesson the teacher discussed that week. PBL would include a community project where students have to stop at three businesses in their community, ask them a problem they've been experiencing, and have the student come up with solutions to those three problems. Students could use the information they've learned for the project from all the lessons and units that have been covered so far.

In shorter projects, students are applying material they've

learned. While PBL also includes material learned, it includes using the project itself as means for delivering education. Instead of students listening to lectures and taking a quiz for a lesson, they would do the project and learn from their experiences.

PBL allows students to learn in a non-traditional way. They can express themselves and take a break from the monotonous routines of school and coursework. PBL can be more fun for students and can increase their learning because the information is relevant and tangible. Tangible, in the sense that they can grasp the information as they are using it.

Unlike shorter projects, students must do more than just remember information. They have to use higher thinking skills and work with others to create solutions and answers.

PROJECT DESIGN

When designing a project, it's important to include aspects of PBL to ensure it doesn't turn into a more common project. There are seven important parts of PBL: problem, inquiry, authenticity, student expression, reflection, revisions and feedback, and product.

A problem should be challenging and meaningful. The questions should be appropriate for the age and education level of students. A question or problem should be interesting and thought-provoking. Children should be excited about the project. Ensure the problem is relevant. This is going to keep the students' attention.

The authenticity of the project is included in real-world problems. Authenticity requires the use of tools and tasks, standards, and issues related to the students' lives and academic careers.

Students should have a voice and a choice in their projects. When students make decisions about their projects, they can choose what they create and how they work. Students will gain more from PBL when expressing their ideas, thoughts, and beliefs.

Reflection is important for students to think back on what they learned. Students can reflect on the effectiveness of their work and activities, quality, and obstacles that they encountered. Students should reflect on the strategies they used for overcoming their problems.

Including feedback in PBL means students can give and receive feedback. Students can receive critiques and use them to revise and improve their products. Feedback can be given to the student via a teacher or other students.

Having a final project gives students the opportunity to see the fruits of their labor. This product can be shown to other students, teachers, or people in the community. PBL means students take pride in what they have accomplished because it was such a personal journey.

You can team up with other teachers, school employees, or community members to create projects to improve learning in the classroom. Motivation for project ideas can come from other experts in the field, videos, online, other students, curriculum, and more.

One of the most important parts of PBL is ensuring that the project is relevant to the curriculum. The project should be personal and fun, but it should also be important and related to a student's studies.

STRATEGIES FOR PBL

It can be daunting to make the switch from traditional content delivery to a PBL based approach. When teachers are making the changes, they can use many teaching practices to promote PBL in the classroom.

Teachers can create a project and adapt it to their students. Teachers will design and plan the project so that students get some degree of choice and voice. When planning the project, make sure you manage and supervise it from the launch stage to the finish.

When creating the project, connect it with academic standards. The project should address understanding and knowledge from subject areas covered in class. Projects should, however, act as a stand-alone lesson. It can be built from other lessons but should include a lesson of its own.

When using PBL, teachers should promote open-ended questions, teamwork, and attention to detail and quality. Promoting growth and independence among students is going to help the student be successful.

Teachers will work together with students to manage

activities. Teachers should work with students to organize schedules and tasks, set deadlines and check-ins, use and find resources, and finally create products to make public.

A variety of tools, strategies, and lessons can support all students. When students have support, they're more likely to reach the goals of the project. The project should set the student up to learn something new.

Assessment of student learning is important for determining progress and how well the students are accepting and working with the project. Summative and formative assessments are conducted by teachers to determine success, understanding, and knowledge. Students can also take part in individual and team assessments.

During PBL implementation, teachers should engage with and coach students. Teachers can work and learn alongside students. Teachers can guide, redirect, celebrate, and encourage student decisions.

AFTER SCHOOL PROGRAMS

It's been proven that social-emotional learning is beneficial for helping students manage emotions, create good relationships, avoid negative behaviors, and make appropriate decisions. New studies show that providing at-risk students with an after-school program improves social and emotional skills. It was shown that academic performance and behavior in the classroom improved after attending an after-school program.

The students who were a part of the program had an increased self-awareness, didn't bully, and had less conflict with others. After-school programs have been shown to build confidence, make the students excited to learn, allow for supervision and safety, and create a feeling of belonging.

You can get the most benefits from SEL when it is both inside and outside of the classroom. Integrating SEL into different parts of students' lives allows them to view it in a number of situations through different perspectives.

An after-school program can give students something to look forward to during the week. Not all students have good home lives, so providing them with an after-school program can improve their confidence and their chances of being successful in life.

These programs can show students the importance of school and where it can take them in their lives. Students may also get to experience content that they wouldn't have otherwise in the classroom. They will also build bonds and relationships with the other students in the program.

The community can also benefit from after-school programs because they can pair with the group to create and finish projects. A local after-school program could be made for children to volunteer to do things around town, such as picking up trash or painting an old building. This also gives students the opportunity to build their resumes and expertise.

One great way to take full advantage of after-school programs is to implement technology. There are digital services that aim to connect many students regardless of location. You can use technology to expose your students to various cultures and mindsets. This is going to make them more understanding and empathetic adults. This also improves the students' team-building and conflict resolution skills. Students are able to discuss with each other their topics and find common ground.

The Internet plays a large role in connecting people from all over the world. Online collaboration on cloud-based services allows multiple people to interact with information at a time. Changes can be tracked in real-time and are organized and shown by each person who makes an edit or addition.

7

TAKING ACTION

*D*esign thinking is a tool for teachers to use when creating a classroom for kids to think deeply and work through interdisciplinary challenges. Design thinking means adopting a mindset that focuses on processes that promote student independence and success. Design thinking includes finding ways to incorporate UDL and SEL in the classroom.

The popularity of design thinking has grown over the past few years. While more teachers are learning design thinking, more students are becoming successful in the classroom. The great part of design thinking means it can be customized for your own contexts and situations.

Design thinking offers an opportunity for teachers to come together and work towards improving school culture for students. This creates a network of support from other teachers and school officials. There are four major parts of design thinking you want to choose when defining your approach: empathy, challenging assumptions, experimenting, and sharing the process.

Empathy is critical to human-centered design. Leading with empathy means you are about to see situations and reality through the eyes and perceptions of others. Teachers are successful when leading with empathy because they understand the causes of the situations we are in and the needs of others.

When leading with empathy, listen to others more and talk less. Place yourself in the mindset of those who experience you or your program. This is going to give you a critical mindset that you can use to evaluate your program.

Challenging assumptions means making the best decision when you're faced with conflict. Assumptions are what is normally done. Challenging assumptions means you are looking for ways to make things better. You're not accepting of how things have always been. You want to change the world and do that by searching for ways to help.

Use the language of possibility. Using phrases such as "What if..." and "How..." These phrases are going to open minds to the suggestion of making changes. Find ways that you can make something easier. Do you get the generic answer, "That's just how it is"? If so, challenge how it's done and see what you can do differently.

Experimenting means you try something and learn whether it works or not. When you're taking action, you have to experiment with different situations and solutions. You can try different options to see what can work for your situation.

Instead of constantly talking about how to solve a problem, create a list of ways that problem could be solved and try them. Once you've tried something new, observe what happened and reflect on the outcomes to get it right and try again.

Sharing your process ensures that everyone can take part in your leadership and success. Sharing your process means sharing all parts, not just the good parts. You share the troubles you had and what you did that didn't work.

Even if it's just hearing about what happened afterward, being a part of the process is important for everyone. They are able to see the entire process from start to finish. Giving them this opportunity to see the inside of what happens is going to give them experience and a different perspective.

SUPPORT

Change takes more than one person. Whether people are helping directly or indirectly, support is very important and can come from many places. When trying to change the culture of your school, lean on other teachers for support. When you can all work together to create change, the process is going to be easier, faster, and more successful.

Teaching is difficult on its own without trying to change the learning characteristics of your school and classroom.

Teachers have to try to do more with less. When teachers work together, they can benefit themselves, their students, and the school system as a whole. There are many ways that you can support other teachers, and they can support you.

One way to garner support in the school is to create a gift fund. Every so often, the school can take up money to put into the special fund. If a teacher was to go through something emotionally draining, or they're celebrating something special, the special fund can be used to buy a gift for them. This is going to create a sense of community throughout the school. Then, when the time comes, they'll be more willing to support one another.

Support can also come from creating a better work-life balance among teachers. Teachers supporting each other in school is just as important as supporting each other outside of school. Create activities that support wellness, such as walking/running groups, book clubs, and other activities. This creates opportunities among the teachers to bond on deeper levels. This creates a well-rounded relationship. The deeper the friendship, the more supportive you all will be.

Giving backup is going to increase support throughout the school. If you know another teacher is meeting with an angry parent, offer to meet the parent with them. If you're having a rough day, see if someone can cover your bus duty. Helping each other when they need it is going to show support, kindness, and community.

School support is something that comes from the heart. If you're feeling burnt out, think about how you can change your circumstances. Maybe you should teach a different subject, or a different grade level, or even at a different school. You may need to leave the school in order to be happier somewhere else. It's not fair to you or your students if you're unhappy or hesitant about being there. Support change where it's needed. Maybe your favorite coworker needs to switch to a different grade level. It may hurt, but you're going to make all the difference by providing support.

BURNOUT

Taking action can be harder when teachers are burnt out. Burnout can be difficult to notice. Teachers may think they're just tired, or they're adjusting to some changes, or they're just distracted. While these may be true, burnout is one of the leading causes of unhappiness in teachers. Burnout can lead to fatigue, inability to adapt, distractions, depression, frustration, poor work performance, and more.

When you're burnt out, you likely have a short fuse with your superiors and/or coworkers. One small situation can ruin the rest of your day. You might get into an argument with a student or decide to take a few days off. When teachers are burnt out, academic performance in the classroom suffers.

It's not that teachers who are burnt out are bad teachers. It's just that they're fed up with their job and ready for a change. They're tired of working overtime and not getting any appreciation for it. Students can also wear a teacher down to the point they don't like teaching that grade or class anymore.

Burnout is a state of long-term stress that can cause emotional and physical exhaustion, detachment, feelings of ineffectiveness, lack of accomplishment, and cynicism. The Alliance for Excellent Education found that about 500,000 teachers in the U.S. leave the profession each year (Haynes, 2015). Other studies show that 17% will leave teaching in their first year (Gray, Taie, O'Rear, 2015). High teacher burnout leads to high turnover, which can burn out the veteran teachers, creating more burnout.

Teacher burnout affects students, other teachers, the school administration, and more. Teachers are at the core of teaching, and when they're unhappy, it affects the success of all parts of the education system. Educational quality takes a nosedive when teachers are burnt out because it causes the "emergency" teachers to be given certificates to teach. These teachers are sometimes underqualified and even unqualified. Because they are thrown so quickly into teaching, it can lead to higher rates of burnout at an earlier time in their career. These teachers have a 25% higher chance of leaving their school and the profession (Thomas, Hammond, 2017).

There are three types of burnout:

1. Frenetic. Frenetic burnout includes the teachers who have put lots of time and energy into their work. They're extremely dedicated to connecting personal ambitions with teaching and passionate about achievement. Because of this, their personal lives suffer, meaning they cannot get the self-care needed to lighten the effects of their workload.
2. Under-challenged. The under-challenged teachers lack interest and motivation. They only provide superficial effort, and their irritation with lack of acknowledgment and boring routine push them to get other jobs.
3. Worn-out. Some teachers are simply worn out.

They don't have anything else to give the profession. They have to disregard their responsibilities as they become worn out. Lack of power and lack of recognition eventually leads to neglect of their job.

It's important to notice burnout among other teachers, as well as school administrators. Studies have listed symptoms to look for when you suspect a teacher is burnt out.

- The sacrifice of personal time by constant meetings, grading, and classroom preparation.
- An overwhelming feeling of not being able to get their job done, regardless of what they do.
- Unfulfillment in their work.
- Frustration from the inability to make a change, teaching for tests rather than learning, taking away from meaningful time for education, and having to jump through professional hoops.
- Physical and emotional exhaustion from teachers not getting enough sleep.
- Stress from repetitive classroom issues, lack of self-care, lack of support, parents, and tests.
- Physical symptoms of overworking and stress.

Improving teacher burnout requires help from other teachers, administration, students, community, teachers, and support personnel and aides. When all of these people work together, they can create a more successful environment for teachers. One of the best ways to fix teacher burnout includes bringing in more teachers. With the constant demand for more work or changing policies with less help, teachers are struggling. Bringing more teachers into the school allows for smaller workloads and class sizes among teachers.

Giving teachers more control over their daily lives also helps cure teacher burnout. Teachers have the ability to change their classrooms, but they don't always have the opportunity. This could be done by letting teachers have more control over their curriculum. This can also create a stronger sense of community among teachers because they won't feel so micromanaged.

Teacher burnout can be improved by:

- Administering an anonymous survey to attempt to find any hidden problems that could be leading to teacher distress.
- Adding more staff to schools and classrooms.
- Changing policies to allow for more freedom among teachers.
- Providing instruction on beneficial de-stressing techniques and coping mechanisms.
- Giving more support for the teachers' needs.
- Listening to what teachers are saying and trying to say.
- Offering physical and mental health amenities.

- Creating a plan for improving teacher burnout.
- Creating a stronger sense of community among other teachers.

When schools improve teacher burnout, they are better preparing teachers to take action for positive change.

ACTION RESEARCH

Action research is a process done in order to find problems that can be solved by teachers. Action research can take place by a group of colleagues or even the entire staff of a school. Action research is the process of identifying issues that may or may not be visible and what is needed in order to change them. Action research can act as a guide for how to solve problems that teachers may already know about. There are seven steps that makeup action research:

1. Selecting a focus.
2. Clarifying theories.
3. Finding research questions.
4. Collecting data.
5. Analyzing data.
6. Reporting results.
7. Taking informed action.

Step one is the beginning of the action research process.

In step one, you select a focus. This means you are going to find a topic that is worthy enough for a teacher's time. Teachers are so overworked and stressed, so finding a topic that's important to the teacher is going to be the most beneficial. Teachers can't afford to waste time on silly aspects. During step one, you are going to decide what you want to investigate.

Step two involves clarifying theories. This means discovering the beliefs, theoretical perspectives, and values of the teacher or team. After deciding what topic to discuss, step two includes how you are going to approach the topic. If teachers value leadership in the classroom, focus on how you want to improve leadership among students. You can also target the values of the students in order to make them more receptive to your message.

In step three, you are going to want to find your research questions. These questions are going to guide your research. What are you trying to figure out, specifically? Do you just have a broad question you want to answer? You can have multiple research questions, but having too many at once can get confusing. It's best if you stick to a few simple questions. This way, resources aren't being divided between multiple topics, and more effort can go into one question.

Next is step four. After you have your focus, values, and beliefs in check and your research question, it's time to collect data. You have done everything up to this point to get you ready to find research. It's important to do steps one through three first because they are going to give you a more specific idea of what to research.

When being in the field of education, it's very important for teachers and staff to stay up to date on new instructional designs and ideas. With the classroom becoming more and more diverse and teachers needing to give more and more, instructional design is going to change as we move into the future. This shows why it is important to have valid research data. Research data can come from multiple sources, but it is important to understand the credibility of those sources.

One great way to collect data is to use multiple sources of information. The commonalities between multiple sources of information can identify common ideas throughout that field of study. For example, if you find evidence that leadership skills can improve academic performance in children from multiple sources, chances are higher that that is correct, or at least an important idea. This is called triangulation.

Triangulation means using multiple pieces of information to increase the reliability and validity of the research. Imagine researching a topic that's inside a box. You have to look through multiple windows to see the inside of the box. From each window, you have a different view of the topic. Moving around from window to window is an example of triangulation. Gathering information from various areas gives researchers the ability to compare and contrast what is being said about that topic.

Finding research to use in the class doesn't mean that it

will succeed. Even if it is research-proven, it might fail your students. When collecting data, focus on processes that are going to fit your students. Some teachers can be intimidated by the idea of data collection. It can sound tedious and scary. However, there are areas of research every day in the classroom. The ways students interact with each other can give you inspiration on what to research.

Write down the questions that your students ask you and you can't answer. What are some things you've seen in the classroom that have interested you? You don't have to spend hours slumped in front of your computer scrolling through countless websites and articles. Simply pay attention to the information flowing around you in everyday life.

Step five starts with analyzing data. Now that you've read all of this research and you have highlights and stickies everywhere, it's time to organize it and find patterns. This is the part in action research where you will examine, sort, rank, and sift their data to answer their research questions. Are there common patterns in research? Is there conflicting evidence between sources?

This may be an area where you decide to do more research. If you feel like none of your information fits together, you may need to reevaluate your research question and ask yourself what different information you can gather. You should have your data together when it's time to report the results. Looking at all of your information together may also create more questions that you want to answer.

In step six, you report the results. Many times, in teacher-led action research, reporting the results is an informal process. You can report your results to other colleagues, school administrations, parents, etc. You can also type up your research and have it published. This is where you take pride in your work and get excited about showing others.

Step seven includes action planning. This is where you use the research you completed to implement it into everyday practices. Use what you found to make your classroom and your students better. Once you have the results, you're going to be able to think about all of the ways you can use this information. Take action on your research so you can spread your valuable work.

CONFIDENCE

With the constant pressure put on teachers, it can be hard to build confidence. Students can act out and make teachers feel as though they can't reach them. Teachers also get discouraged when they can't do everything that's asked of them by the school and students. This leads to frustration and a dive in self-confidence. In the constant path of struggle, teachers have to be confident in themselves to take action to make a change.

As a teacher, it can be easy to focus on all of the bad instead of all of the good. This is because the bad parts of teaching are more emotionally memorable than the good times. Plus, you're going to be able to see the bad parts a lot more often than the good parts. Teachers are constantly making a difference in their students; they just may not be able to see it right now. A few years down the road, the student is going to be using the information you taught them.

Hearing how positively influential teachers can be, make it hard to believe that teachers can have low self-confidence. Teachers owe it to themselves to be confident, so they can demand the respect they deserve.

Confidence is vital to making a change in education. Teachers experience enough pushback without actively trying to make a change. Making a change in education starts in the classroom. But what happens when you're wildly successful? What about when other teachers and students hear about something really cool you've implemented in your classroom?

Now, let's say the school or administration thinks you should go back to the way it was. It's time to challenge the norm! If you've created a new idea in your classroom and it's getting popular, why wouldn't you share it with others? Lack of self-confidence can deter teachers away from sharing their ideas with others. Fear of reprimand or embarrassment can keep instructors from sharing their findings.

One way for teachers to build self-confidence includes:

- Creating a group among other teachers to talk about confidence. Having a group of support at your disposal can provide you with the confidence boost to make changes.

- Welcoming criticism. Criticism is considered the scary, hateful information that includes our flaws and downfalls. Look at criticism as an opportunity to better yourself. Without criticism, you may never find out how you can get better.

- Be prepared for negative interactions. Some students can be very rude and take a lot of misplaced emotions out on teachers. This is a prime opportunity for self-doubt to grow in teachers. Remember that these students are going through many changes in their lives right now. Their reactions may have nothing to do with you, even if they are directing their attitude towards you. Be secure in yourself and stand tall in the face of adversity.

- Find your strengths. Even if your strengths aren't necessarily associated with teaching (maybe you're a really great swimmer), it's important to keep them in mind and learn from them. Did you push yourself to break a personal record last week? Remember the motivation and drive you used to excel in your personal goal. Use that attitude to persevere.

- Learn more about yourself. When you're unsure of yourself, you're unsure of your actions. You're going to second guess yourself. It's going to be hard to trust yourself. Learn more about who you are and what you're about. When you have a better understanding of yourself, you're going to be more secure. Being secure means being confident.

Not only will confidence help create change in the class-room, but it will also motivate other teachers to gain confidence to join you in making a difference.

8

MAKING A REMARKABLE TEACHER

*E*very teacher, at one point, aspires to be the best teacher they know. They want to change the lives of others and educate them to better themselves. It is truly an honor to be a teacher because whether you think it or not, you have a long-lasting impact on someone's life.

It can be nerve-wracking trying to create change in your school community. You may be afraid of embarrassment from others. It can be scary to take the first step into change. It's hard to know who is going to stick it out with you until the end. You just have to create a mindset that allows you to be open to change.

When you're open to change, you're more likely to persevere. This isn't to say that you won't reach obstacles or get tired and frustrated. This just means you're going to have the time and energy to overcome these problems.

Every teacher is different. Every educational environment is different. However, according to Azer (2005), there are certain qualities that are common among great teachers.

- Be committed to your work. The best teachers will put a focus on the needs of the students. They work with passion and want to uphold the school's values. The greatest teachers are enthusiastic about teaching and their work.
- Encouragement and appreciation for diversity are common in exceptional teachers. They don't act on stereotypes or speak inappropriately of others. They encourage and nurture diversity. Teachers who are great will encourage others to respect people regardless of their backgrounds.
- You're going to find great teachers who communicate and interact with respect. They have strong communication skills, listen intently, and act with integrity. These teachers encourage input from others and display a caring attitude. You can see remarkable teachers modeling high ethical standards.
- Motivation is one of the important characteristics of being a memorable teacher. Providing constructive feedback is a given when dealing with amazing teachers. Greatness is shown when teachers foster the success of students and monitor their progress.

- Talent and skills are important for being a good teacher. High-order thinking skills are clearly presented in these teachers. Teachers should be memorable and bring strong evidence when critiquing work.
- Being a leader is very beneficial to be a remarkable teacher. Leadership in teaching means contributing to education, publications, structure, and course design. Leadership means showing self-development, whether it's in personal life or in an educational environment. These teacher leaders show creativity when engaging in teaching techniques. Teachers who are leaders are dedicated to professional development in the education field.
- Creating a trusting and open learning environment shows signs of a good teacher. These teachers will create trust, motivate students to learn from their mistakes, and use failure as an opportunity for learning. An amazing teacher allows student questions and engagement. Teachers should improve student growth using behavior-based feedback.
- A quality teacher will foster critical thinking. Students will learn how to think instead of what to think. Students are encouraged to analyze, organize, and evaluate information to learn. Teachers can benefit from using probing questions, organizing ideas for discussion, and

helping students find and focus on important issues. Students also greatly benefit from teachers by learning strategic thinking.

- Great teachers encourage creativity, motivate the students to create their own ideas, and foster a strong environment for new approaches and innovation.
- In order to be an exceptional teacher, you must emphasize teamwork. These teachers can create links and national and international organizations in education. They encourage teamwork among students and stress the importance of collaborative learning.
- Great teachers want to keep improving. They want to learn and use new skills and stay up to date in their field. Seeking feedback and criticism is what brings these teachers to a new level.
- Lastly, these teachers give positive feedback. They listen to their students and find their educational needs. They support the growth of students, value them, and never belittle students. They teach students to keep track of their own progress and success.

To wrap it up, some of the best qualities in a teacher are (Azer, 2005):

1. Commitment
2. Appreciating and encouraging diversity
3. Respect
4. Motivation
5. Skills and talent
6. Leadership
7. Trust
8. Improving critical thinking
9. Creative
10. Being a team-player
11. Providing positive feedback

Some of these qualities are innate, but many can be learned. Using a positive mindset will make it easier to acquire these qualities.

POSITIVE MINDSET

Having a positive mindset can not only improve your teaching skills, but it can build confidence and improve your whole life. When you learn to adopt a positive mindset, you'll never view something the same again.

Having a positive mindset changes your life because you use failures as a lesson and optimism as a general rule. Studies show that positive thinking can have physical and mental benefits. Positive mindsets can lead to higher confidence and better moods. Positive thinking can prevent the chances of developing certain conditions like depression, anxiety, and hypertension.

It can be hard to completely change to positive thoughts, but it's feasible. Having a positive mindset means changing your perspective. Changing your perspective can change everything about the way you see various situations and events. You can find the good in everything and cling to it instead of allowing the negative to beat you down. If something is already done, and it cannot be changed, there is no need to dwell on it. You must change the way you see the situation and move forward from it. Otherwise, it will claim you.

In order to create a positive mindset, start your day with positive affirmations. Your morning can determine how the rest of your day will go. If you wake up late and anxious, then your entire day is going to feel rushed and annoying. Have you had one bad situation, and it seems like it's ruined your entire day? Starting your day with positive affirmations means standing in the mirror and telling yourself, "Today will be great" or "I am going to do awesome." It may feel silly, but you'll be surprised how much it can help.

The saying, "Every storm cloud has a silver lining," can be so annoying to hear. No one wants to hear, "But just focus on the good" when we are distressed. It's normal to feel anger and anxiety for a short time after a situation. However, it can be debilitating if these emotions follow you for hours, days, weeks, or longer. Once you realize these negative emotions are taking over your feelings, try to change your perspective to focus on the "silver lining."

The good in a bad situation can be very small. Such as attending a divorce mediation, but there's free coffee. Or being in traffic for an hour, but at least you can listen to a great podcast. Or the vending machine is out of your favorite snack, so you have to try something new instead. If you like it, then you've just found a great new snack! If you hate it, now you know you don't like it, so you won't get it again (at this point, just pack your lunch).

Finding humor in tough situations can really help the way you see what's happening. Understand those tough situations will not last forever, and viewing them with humor can change your outlook. If you get lost driving home, at least you took the scenic route. Think about how you can, appropriately, joke about the situation.

Lessons should come from failure. Failure can put a damper on our confidence, mood, performance, etc. When you fail, you are simply learning what didn't work. Take advantage of this new information and use it in the future. Use this information to prevent making the same mistake again.

We are all victims of negative self-talk. We scold ourselves for grabbing a donut while on a diet or beat ourselves up for being late to work. It can be hard to notice our self-talk. It is second nature to us, and we can mold our behavior, thoughts, and actions based on our inner critic.

Negative thoughts can turn to negative feelings and negative perceptions. So, even if something isn't really that bad, we are going to think it is. When you notice you're being negative, try to use positive self-talk. Instead of saying, "I'm awful at this," instead try, "With some practice, I can be great." It is the same situation but from different perspectives.

Be present in your thoughts and actions. A lot of anxiety is the thought of what could happen next. When you're focused on the now, it's going to be harder for you to visualize the negative future. Many negative thoughts can come from memories or fears of the future. When you're focused on the present, you can realize that things may not be as bad as we make them seem.

Having positive friends, family, and coworkers can also help you be a more positive person. They will be able to give you ways to be more positive and show you how to see situations differently. These positive people can act as a support group when you need them the most. Practicing with your group can benefit your life and theirs.

Having a positive mindset is going to allow you to have an easier transition through making a change. You're going to be more confident about the next step. You can learn from failures and thrive in bad situations. You can use humor when you're scared and positive self-talk when you're being mean to yourself. Having a positive mindset will allow you to be more patient and positive during change and implementation.

CONCLUSION

First, we discussed the toxic culture of education. We bring light to problems that are blanketed across schools nation-wide. From standardized testing to the GPA and ranking system, you understand how these issues are affecting education and student performance. If students can't seem to overcome these obstacles, they could be deemed a "failure." However, we went on to discuss the teacher's influence and what it takes to change. There are problems, but we under-stand, now, that we can change them.

Now, the highlight of the book: equity and its impor-tance. Equity is so important because it provides everyone the attention they need to be successful. Equality means giving everyone the same thing. Equity means giving each child what they need to succeed, regardless of if it's more than others. Children with learning disabilities could get private study lessons. While this isn't technical equality, it is providing these students with the same opportunities to succeed as their peers. Keep note of the steps towards achieving equity. This is important for you to create an equitable environment in your classroom and your school.

Listening and hearing aren't the same thing. Teachers have a unique opportunity to be the sun in a solar system of stakeholders. They can see administration, community, family, school, and family all at once. It can be overwhelming and exhausting to be at the center of everyone and everything in education. However, when teachers can take the time to listen, they are going to be able to effectively get information from those around them. They may learn about other situations of which they were not aware. They are also the go-to person when a child needs help. Listening as a teacher is important and can change the lives of your students.

One of the lengthiest but critical parts of the book talks about social-emotional learning. The book covers SEL so thoroughly because it is very beneficial to the development of students. SEL can improve quality of life as well as academic performance. We explained the pillars of social-emotional learning and the difference between EQ and IQ. The problem is that standardized tests, GPAs, and the ranking system will rank kinds based on IQ. It does not account for EQ which can be just as important.

Creating an SEL program can seem intimidating, but you can do it with information and dedication. You've learned how to determine if your program was successful and what can be done differently in order to create a more effective program. Be on the lookout for pitfalls as they can interfere with improving SEL in students. We finish up chapter 4, discussing how SEL can be used in college and careers.

Universal design learning (UDL) includes representation, action and expression, and engagement. UDL and implementation can be done in all classrooms and schools. Using UDL in the classroom gives the students more opportunities to learn and excel through experience. Chapter 5 also explains implementation programs for UDL.

Now that you've covered the background information and explanations, it's time to take action. You've found strategies and plans that are going to help you to create a change in the educational world. Chapter 6 discusses technology and how it can be used for education. However, distraction can happen with technology, so we covered some tips on working through and avoiding digital distractions.

We move onto techniques for building equity. You have the background; now, you need to know how you can build equity. Building equity allows all students the opportunity to express themselves and learn more about themselves. Expression and self-exploration can take place in project-based learning. Project-based learning allows students to learn topics and subjects from real life rather than a lecture. Lastly, some strategies and plans are included regarding after-school programs and how they're important.

The book shows how to take action. Support can be one

of the greatest ways to achieve change. Fighting for change can be scary and even lonely. Support can come in and help hold us when we need it. Having a support system is how we can avoid burnout. Burnout affects teachers all over the world and inhibits them from doing what they love to the best of their abilities.

On more of the educational aspect, action research is taking the chance to learn about problems in your school. You can research how prevalent this problem is and how some people have, or haven't, solved the problem. You can find ways that work and implement them into your study. Once you have compiled your information, you can report your findings with confidence and clarity. Confidence is very important for taking and implementing change.

Last, we talked about how to be an amazing teacher. Every school, teacher, student, and classroom is different. What may work for one teacher will not work for the other. Being a remarkable teacher means using some of the qualities we discussed before since these are common in a lot of great teachers. Adopting a positive mindset will help you change your life, not only in your academic life but also in your personal life. Being positive is going to keep you strong in the face of trouble.

If you're taking time to learn more about equity and being a good teacher, you care about yourself, your jobs, and your students. You want to take pride in your work and set an example for those watching you and following you. Being a good teacher starts with educating yourself on problems and providing the resources students need to overcome obstacles that stand between them and a solid education. Let's go and change education!

Consider joining our Facebook group "Equity In Education: Community For Teachers," where you will find more educators like you supporting each other, sharing ideas, and helping to make education better one step at a time. Here is the link: https://www.facebook.com/groups/equityineducationcommunity

If you have enjoyed this book, please leave us a review on Amazon to help more teachers find this book and make a massive change in education worldwide.

Scan this QR code to leave a review

RESOURCES

Azer, S. (2005). The qualities of a good teacher: How can they be acquired and sustained? Journal of the Royal Society of Medicine. 98(2): 67–69.

Blad, E. (2017, June 20). Students' Sense of Belonging at School is Important. It Starts With Teachers. Education-Week. https://www.edweek.org/leadership/students-sense-of-belonging-at-school-is-important-it-starts-with-teachers/2017/06#disqus_tread_anchor

Grya, L., Taie, S., O'Rear, I. (2015). Public school teacher attrition and mobility in the first five years: Results from the first through fifth waves of the 2007-08 beginning teacher longitudinal study. U.S. Department of Education. https://nces.ed.gov/pubs2015/2015337.pdf

Haynes, M. (17 July 2014). On the path to equity: Improving the effectiveness of beginning teachers. Alliance for Excellent Education. https://all4ed.org/reports-factsheets/path-to-equity/

Segool, N., Carlson, J., Goforth, A., Embse, N., Barterian, J. (2013). Heightened test anxiety among young children: elementary school students' anxious responses to high stakes testing. Psychology in the Schools, 50(5), 489 - 499. https://doi.org/10.1002/pits.21689

Thomas, D., Hammond, L. (2017). Teacher turnover: Why it matters and what we can do about it. Palo Alto, CA: Learning Policy Institute.